DILNAWAR

— The Last Emperor —

MW00439816

DILIP KUMAR
— The Last Emperor —

Sanjit Narwekar

Rupa & Co

Design Copyright © Rupa & Co. 2006
Text © Sanjit Narwekar 2006

Published in 2006 by

Rupa . Co

7/16, Ansari Road, Daryaganj
New Delhi 110 002

Sales Centres :
Allahabad Bangalore Chandigarh Chennai
Hyderabad Jaipur Kathmandu
Kolkata Mumbai Pune

All rights reserved.
No part of this publication may be reproduced, stored in a retrieval system,
or transmitted in any form or by any means, electronic, mechanical, photocopying,
recording or otherwise, without the prior permission of the publishers.

Cover & Book Design by
Kapil Gupta
kapilkgupta@hotmail.com

Printed in India by
Nutech Photolithographers,
C-74, Okhla Industrial Area, Phase-I.
New Delhi-110 020

— Contents —

– *Prologue* –

Dilip Kumar. Raj Kapoor. Dev Anand. Their names are inseparable in the pantheon of Indian stars. They are all timeless stars who have defied age and changing tastes. They were born within a year of each other (1923/24) and made their debuts within a couple of years of each other: Dilip Kumar in 1944 (with Jwar Bhata), Dev Anand in 1946 (with Hum Ek Hain) and Raj Kapoor in 1947 (with Neelkamal). They were destined to "rule" the Hindi film industry for the next quarter-of-a-century and in the process give a new definition to the concept of stardom in post-Independent India.

Two of them went on to form their own production companies – Raj Kapoor launched R.K.Films in 1948 and Dev Anand launched Navketan in 1951 – and were thus in a position to shape their images and careers. Dilip Kumar, on the other hand, preferred to remain an actor first and last, thus compelled to shape his career and form his image through the "outside" films that he starred in.

This apparent disadvantage actually worked out to his advantage because, right through his career, he got to work with the best of Indian filmmakers in the best of films. Shorn of the responsibility of running a production company and directing a film, he could concentrate on his performances and hone his talent to razor sharp perfection. His power of selection also stood him in good stead.

In film after film, with a few minor cosmetic alterations, he played the tragic brooding introvert who invariably loses his lady-love in the last reel. And, sometimes even his life! Dilip Kumar's tragic screen persona became a role model for other actors who were required to play similar roles and continues to be till this day. His constant foray into tragic roles and his assuming the mantle of the Tragedy King necessitated his taking psychiatric advice, which led to his taking up lighter roles, which he played with equally consummate artistry. Even his character roles created new highs: his was always the pivotal role.

When compared to his contemporaries his output has been meagre. This was in keeping with his policy to ration himself and work only in the best projects – a policy which, in theory, was the correct one since he believed that an artiste must seek to consolidate his work as an actor rather than increase his output. In practice, it did not work out well since it did not get him the expected rewards. But the flops never upset his rhythm or his dedication to the Muse.

Though the output is small, there is no denying that the quality of each one of his performances is to be marvelled at and repeatedly studied as the Actor's Bible. He may have played the same role again and again but he took care to see that the characters were well delineated, right down to the last nuance. It is no wonder therefore that many actors have chosen to model themselves on him and many of them have even made it in the tough world of films in their own right. He has never looked down on such actors nor ever derided them. Instead he has looked upon them as equal partners in an endeavour to create a less artificial cinema.

He had made a foray into production and though the film was a great success the experience was so bitter that he did not find it worth repeating. He took up direction but the film was never completed to his satisfaction probably because the producer could not match his desire for creating true art on celluloid. Maybe he should have stuck to what he does best: Acting.

It's been more than a decade since Dilip Kumar has acted in a film. Maybe he will never act again for he is already in his eighties. But then stranger things have happened .... This then is the story of a man who blazed a histrionic trail, which many actors dreamt of emulating but very few could even follow and none could really emulate.

Chapter One

– *Life in the Frontier City* –

Peshawar, meaning "The Place At The Frontier", was so named by King Akbar because of its proximity to the Khyber Pass, which, for centuries, had been the vantage point as a gateway for the invaders of the sub-continent. Earlier, the city had been variously known as the "City of Flowers", the "City of Grain" and the "Lotus Land". In fact, it has had as many names as rulers.

Founded over 2,000 years ago by the Kushan Kings of Gandhara, it was the centre of the Buddhist Gandhara civilisation and an important place of pilgrimage. It was then known as "Pushpapura" or "the City of Flowers" or even "the Lotus Land". As the influence of Buddhism declined, Peshawar was lost in obscurity till the Mughal King Babur returned to rebuild the fort and city in 1530. His grandson King Akbar improved upon its fortifications and gave the city its modern name. His successor Sher Shah Suri brought Peshawar sharply into focus when he built the Delhi-to-Kabul Shahi Road through the Khyber Pass.

Though the old city wall and the gates no longer exist today, they were very much in evidence less than a century ago when our story begins. Inside the walled city of Old Peshawar were a criss-cross of small streets, bazaars and mohallas. Lying on the apex of the triangle formed between the Kabuli Gate and Asamai Gate is the Mohalla Khodadad in the Kissa Khwani (The Square of Storytellers) Bazaar area, not too far from the Chowk Yaadgar (The Square of Remembrance) and the Clock Tower.

Peshawar is known to have the healthiest climate in this part of the world but during winter the mercury touches a low of 4 degrees Centigrade. On one such bitter-cold day of December 11, 1922 was born Mohammad Yusuf Khan, the third son and fifth child of fruit merchant Ghulam Sarwar Khan and Ayesha Begum. Preceding him were a sister Sakina (later to be known as Apaji) and two bothers Noor Mohammad and the physically ailing Ayub. The fourth child – a girl – had passed away in early childhood.

As a child he was often addressed as "Lale", which is surprising because he was not the youngest child. Other children had followed after his birth but the one who came closest to his vocation was Nasir, born immediately after Yusuf, and who went on to become a popular actor in his own right.

Ghulam Sarwar Khan came from a devout deeply religious Muslim family, which offered the **namaz** five times a day and the ritualistic **namaaz-e-zohar** on Fridays at the local mosque (most probably the Qasim Ali Mosque). As a toddler Yusuf was so plump and heavy that his slow walking would delay everyone on their way to the mosque. So, his father would simply "pick him up like a sack of flour" and complete the distance.

On reaching the mosque, Yusuf would be put aside so that his father could perform the **vazoo**. During the winter months the pond next to mosque would be frozen and the ice had to be broken to get at the chilled water beneath. When his face was washed, Yusuf's face would turn red and numb and often his chapped lips would begin to bleed. And yet, without a murmur, he would imitate his father, step by step, during the **vazoo** and **namaz** sessions.

By all accounts Yusuf was a restless and mischievous child and got into more than his share of scrapes – which is suprising since he grew up into an introspective brooding boy and man. One of Yusuf's favourite childhood pastime was to jump on his grandfather's back for a horse-ride. In play, Yusuf would often yank on the old man's beard in order to get "the horse" to move faster. His grandfather Haji Mohammad Khan was a strict disciplinarian and ran the family with an iron rod. The venerable old gentleman would subject himself to this indignity for the sake of his grandson – much to the astonishment of the ladies, his grandmother and grandaunts, of the house. One day he probably yanked the beard a little too hard and was rewarded with several hard whacks. The horse-rides ended after that.

The summer months were as hot as the winter months were cold with the mercury touching a dizzying 41 degrees Centigrade. During the afternoons the ladies of the house with the children would retire to the cooler **tehkhana** (basement) to sleep through the heat. Yusuf was not interested in sleeping when so many exciting things were happening all around the city. When the ladies had nodded off to sleep he would quietly slip out to roam the bazaars and **mohallas**, picking up forbidden fruit from neighbourhood trees and generally imbibing the hectic life of a frontier town.

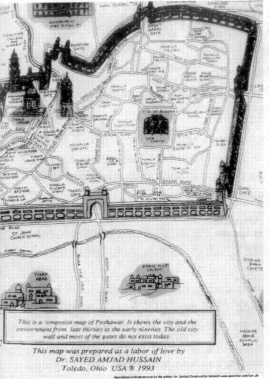

This is a composite map of Peshawar. It shows the city and the enviorment from late thirties to the early nineties. The old city wall and most of the gates do not exist today.

This map was prepared as a labor of love by
Dr. SAYED AMJAD HUSSAIN
Toledo, Ohio USA ® 1993

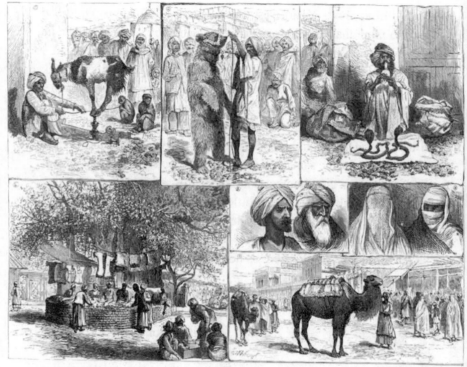

Some impressions of life in the walled city of Peshawar

The streets were lined with shops selling all manner of wares and the quaint Qehwa Khanas or the traditional teashops meant for weary travellers. The style, the decor, the **hookahs** (smoking pipes), and brass samovars with colourful China teapots and small bowls of matching colours would be same at all Qehwa Khana. The tea being served steaming hot, without milk, as it is not the usual black type but has leaves of bottle green colour which gives it its name: green tea.

Life in the frontier province during the 1920s must have been tough. Given its strategic location, its main road being a link between Afghanistan and India, the city was always full of strangers who were given to violent fights. One day, during one such forbidden afternoon sojourn Yusuf caught sight of two Pathan boys with long sticks, playing a peculiarly violent game. They were hitting each other so as to draw blood. The boys must have been fighting for quite some time because their clothes were soaked in blood. This was probably the first time that young Yusuf had seen blood. The sight chilled him to the marrow of his bones and he ran back to the safety of the **tehkhana**.

In another incident he remembers returning from his uncle's shop situated at Kabuli Gate when whistles and shouts pierced through the air. Suddenly there was a stampede and he realised that the British soldiers had started firing. He quietly slipped behind the wall of a house and waited for the panic to end. Just then a British soldier grabbed him by the collar and pulled him out of his hiding place, giving him a painful slap across his face. Yusuf ran away as fast his legs could carry him to his house.

Once the neighbourhood was rent with the mournful cries of women. A wayward truck had crushed the three young sons of a neighbour who was mourning her loss. Yusuf's mother Ayesha Begum had joined the group of mourning women and naturally Yusuf was with her. This went on till the police arrived to take away the bodies for a post mortem – something which the neighbours would not allow. Tempers ran high and daggers were drawn. The police resorted to firing. Yusuf slipped under the bed to hide from the confusion. Once the problem was resolved and quiet had returned, he looked around and discovered that he had taken refuge under the bed with the three badly mutiliated bodies. This incident really shook him up.

Maybe it was the quick-tempered Pathan blood which made violence a part of the 1920s Peshawar. Or maybe it had something to do with the fact that the city was a frontier town where there always was a floating population of adventurers and ruffians. Chacha Gani was a popular figure with the children. He was an orchadsman employed by Sarwar Khan to look after his extensive orchards because he himself would often be travelling to market his goods. One day the boys saw Chacha Gani chained to a tree. The man seemed downcast and forlorn and refused to meet their eyes. As the days went by Chacha Gani became weaker and weaker and eventually passed away. The boys were devastated.

What had Chacha Gani done to deserve this fate they wanted to know? Sarwar Khan explained that Chacha Gani would often enter the orchards on full moon nights and slit the throats of unsuspecting people who had entered the orchards to enjoy a quiet night. The sight of flowing blood gave him a strange thrill. Soon this habit became an obsession and there was a hue and cry. Eventually Chacha Gani had asked to be chained to the tree so that he could be prevented from further crimes.

Such was the Peshawar that young Yusuf grew up in and it undoubtedly provided the angst that was necessary to play the roles that he was to play in the years to come. But Fate was to play a hand in the affairs of the young boy and take him far away from his violent neighbourhood to gentler surroundings. One day his elder brother Ayub Khan was thrown off a horse and severely injured his backbone. Local doctors recommended that he be shown to the topmost surgeon in Bombay, Dr V.L.Parmar. Sarwar Khan already had a wholesale fruit shop at the Crawford Market in Bombay, which he had to visit quite often. It was, therefore, an easy decision to shift the entire family to Bombay.

Chapter Two

– The Formative Years –

Bombay in the 1930s was already recognized as the commercial capital of India. It was also steadily emerging as the film capital of the country. Sarwar Khan rented premises at Nagdevi Street, situated off Mohammad Ali Road, which was close to his shop at Crawford Market (now known as the Mahatma Jyotiba Phule Market), which is still poised between what was once the British Fort and the local town. It's a blend of Flemish and Norman architecture with a bas relief depicting Indian peasants in wheat fields just above the main entrance. The frieze, incidentally, was designed by Lockyard Kipling, father of the famous writer Rudyard Kipling, and the Kiplings' cottage still stands next to the JJ School of Art across the road.

Dilip Kumar still remembers his first impression of Bombay, "We lived on the fourth floor of a building. I remember it was quite unusual to find ourselves climbing flights and flights of the staircase. Even then the city seemed to be crowded ... **yahan hamesha log pe log rahate the** ... and my mother couldn't adjust herself to the congestion."

But their stay at Bombay was, at best, an interlude, because Dr. Parmar discovered that Bombay's humid climate was not conducive for Ayub's quick recovery. Nor was it conducive for Ayesha Begum. Sarwar Khan was advised to move the family to a dry climate and it was decided that Deolali, 65 kilometres from Nasik, would be the best place to shift to, considering that it also had some of the best schools.

Thus the family migrated to Deolali when Yusuf was six years old. Here he was enrolled at the prestigious Barnes School where he spent more time playing football than studying in class. His father disliked him playing a ruffianly game like football and, instead, wanted him

Crawford Market, 1930

to concentrate on a more intelligent game like chess, which was a favourite game of the Khan family. A compromise was thus worked out: Yusuf would begin playing chess in the early afternoon, substitute his brother in his place and leave for the playing fields and then return to take his place at the chess board. In spite of all this Yusuf never lost his interest in football – eventually becoming the secretary of the school football club.

When the war clouds began to loom on the horizon, Deolali was declared a military cantonment and most of the buildings were taken over by the military or the Government. Sarwar Khan's bungalow was among them. The family had to perforce move once again and this time it was decided to shift back to Bombay where the family took up residence on Pali Mala Road in Bandra, not too far from where Dilip Kumar eventually bought a bungalow. This must have been some time in the middle of 1937. Yusuf must have been 14 years old then and to that day he had not seen a single film – indeed some kind of a record for someone who was to become a film star.

Yusuf and his younger brother Nasir were enrolled at the Anjuman-e-Islam High School opposite the Victoria Terminus Station (now the Chhatrapati Shivaji Terminus) and still close enough from Sarwar Khan's shop at Crawford Market. The Anjuman-e Islam High School at Bombay was originally founded by Badruddin Tyabji to promote Muslim education in the Urdu medium. Yusuf was then on the verge of the matriculation examination. But that did not seem to bother the young lad much because, once again, he shone more on the playing fields than the classroom. Here he befriended another young lad who was to become his most consistent co-star: Mukri. Actually it was Mukri's elder brother who was Yusuf's classmate.

Soon after his matriculation, Yusuf joined the Wilson College in the Science stream because his father wanted him to pursue that subject. Left to himself he was keen on doing Literature. He was not a brilliant student but a studious one. He was keen to bridge the gap between Peshawar, Deolali and Bombay. So he joined the literary society. He would read anything that he could lay his hands on. His voracious reading habit had improved his English and his essays were often cited as examples to emulate.

He was an inconspicuous boy who preferred to keep to himself most of the time. This combination of good English and wanting to remain aloof probably led him to the cinema where he would mostly see Hollywood films. Though serious in nature it was not above him to sneak out of college to attend the afternoon show. As at school, Yusuf was also more inclined towards sports – particularly football. The elitist Wilson College would not allow him to play on its behalf so he played the game professionally: the Khalsa College would even pay him Rs 15 per match appearance. It is said that the Sikh taxi drivers of the area would often gather to watch him play and to cheer him on. Probably the only "negative" aspect of the game was that girls would congregate in large numbers to watch the games.

He was an excruciatingly shy lad who was unwilling to attract attention to himself. So much so that he would even hesitate to pass a group of girls to go to his seat in the classroom. But that did not mean that he was unromantic. Unfortunately most of his romances were silent affairs, which began and ended in his own mind. The girls rarely realised that they were the object of his affections. In any case they must have been passing infatuations of the kind any teenage boy was subject to. At this point neither he nor his younger brother Nasir would have any idea that they would become film stars though his brother was already toying with the idea. Yusuf on the other hand was more eager to join his father's flourishing business and make money. That's all he wanted: make money and keep his family happy.

But then the unthinkable happened: his father's business began to decline. Actually, it was the opposite of what should have happened because anyone who was dealing in commodities during Wartime should have prospered – more so, since Sarwar Khan had that most important of commodities: fruit. But he had no transport since it had been put in the service of Wartime supplies. From sending out four to five wagons a day the business went down to two wagons a week, and it kept getting worse with each passing day.

The fruits started rotting and so, they were made into marmalades and jam but there was still a lot left. Eventually the fruit was distributed to the villagers or just thrown away. The Khans lost heavily in their own orchards as well as those they had contracted. Dilip Kumar remembers those agonising years, "Our business was sold and so were our houses in Peshawar and Deolali. And the ornaments, too, all of them. We could visibly see the distress in the family. My father began to do lesser businesses like dealing in onions but his heart was not in it. So Mr Yusuf Khan had to earn something and contribute to the family kitty."

Dropping out of college Yusuf joined the military contractors Wazir Mohammad & Sons in Poona as Assistant Manager at the princely salary of Rs 36 per month. While there he saw the British officers enter the club with their own baskets of fruits. He sought the owner's permission to open a fruit stall and was granted it. On the very first day he made a profit of Rs 22, nearly two-thirds his monthly salary. Soon he saw another opportunity to sell tea and coffee along with sandwiches on dancing nights. He applied for and was granted permission for that, too. Soon he was making almost a thousand rupees a month. However an ordinance, which allowed only government contractors to sell in the army canteen, brought all this to an end but Yusuf returned home on the day of Eid richer by several thousand rupees.

Chapter Three

– Discovering Films –

Bombay Talkies was one of the three institutions – along with the Prabhat Film Company in Poona and the New Theatres in Calcutta – which had dominated Indian filmmaking since the beginning of the talkie era. Founded by Himansu Rai in 1934, with the support of wealthy financiers like Sir Cowasji Jehangir and Sir Chunilal Mehta, Bombay Talkies was the first public limited film company to be set up in India with its shares being listed on the Bombay Stock Exchange.

The scion of a wealthy Bengali family Himansu Rai had trained at Santiniketan and then as a lawyer in London. Drawn to the newly-emerging medium of cinema, he had blazed a trail during the silent era with a series of films made with British and then, German collaboration. Later, at Bombay Talkies, the height of the Himansu Rai era had witnessed the production of superhits like *Kangan* (Franz Osten/1939), *Bandhan* (N.R.Acharya/ 1940) and *Jhoola* (Gyan Mukerji/1941) – all three Ashok Kumar-Leela Chitnis starrers.

With Himansu Rai's death in 1940 the best years of the company seemed to be behind it. Rai's actress-wife Devika Rani was in charge of production but she seemed to spend all her time making peace between two warring groups in the studio: one led by Amiya Chakraborty and the other led by Sashadhar Mukherji and Rai Bahadur Chunilal. Finally the latter group broke away and started Filmistan in 1942.

The company's top star Ashok Kumar, brother-in-law of S. Mukherji, was on the verge of leaving the studio as were many others since they had thrown their lot with Filmistan and Devika Rani was afraid that the studio which her husband had so painstakingly built would soon vanish into nothingness. She was therefore on the lookout for new faces, which would infuse the studio with new enthusiasm and new ideas.

Yusuf's major ambition in life at that point was to be a Test cricketer, to score a century in a Test match some day. Like most film stars of that era he literally stumbled into films. Yusuf Khan was then assisting his father who continued to deal in fruits but on a commission basis. Recalls Dilip Kumar today, "I was always business-minded and loved the family business. My father grew apricots, grapes, pomegranates, apples and peaches and sold them tinned. He would proudly show me the size of his fruits and say, 'This is what I want you to grow Yusuf. Because you're my most intelligent son.' He wanted me to be educated so I could expand the family business."

But life for the young lad was tough. The entire process – from plucking of fruits to their dispatch – was quite cumbersome and since Sarwar Khan was now too old to travel extensively Yusuf would be sent to the Himalayan region, particularly Dehradun and Nainital to buy fruits on an annual contract basis. During one such visit to Nainital he was introduced to Devika Rani who had come location hunting with director Amiya Chakraborty. She probably liked the look of the tall strapping Pathan and so, instinctively asked him to see her in Bombay. On his return, however, Yusuf forgot about the offer or probably did not take it seriously enough to visit Bombay Talkies, which was in the backwoods of the beyond, in Malad.

What actually motivated him to finally make that visit to the studio is not known but it could have been the realisation that he was not making any headway in his father's business. Besides, the Second World War had also been extremely hard on the horticulture business. So he probably decided to get another job with a decent salary. His younger brother Nasir Khan was then actively toying with the idea of a film career. Acting had never really interested Yusuf but with a little goading and a personal recommendation from Dr Masani (who had once been Himansu Rai's personal physician) he made the trip to Malad and chanced upon S.Guruswamy, the production controller

Devika Rani...in search of new faces

(later with Guru Dutt) sitting in the studio compound eating **kairi** (raw mango). For some reason the studio was closed and Yusuf had to return the next day to meet Devika Rani. The next day's meeting was brief and lasted all of four questions:

"Have you acted in films?"
"No!"
"Would you like to act in films?"
"Yes!"
"Do you smoke?"
"No!"
"Do you speak Urdu?"
"Yes."

The brevity of the answers and the shyness with which they were answered probably raised some doubts in Devika Rani's mind. As Dilip Kumar recalls the occasion, "While in Nainital she had engaged me on the spot but back in Bombay she showed signs of uneasiness about her choice and confessed to the director that I knew nothing about acting." But the director Amiya Chakraborty said that he was satisfied with the boy. Not satisfied and still unsure of her choice she referred the matter to Hiten Chowdhary, who was then just an advisor but soon to take over as Controller of Productions, saying, "He has come with a recommendation from a doctor friend to whom I am obliged."

Chowdhary replied, "It is not possible to judge a person's acting potential by merely looking at him. He will have to go through the usual tests, at least a few of them." Then as an afterthought he added, "If you are obliged to the doctor and your bill amounts to several thousands of rupees you should have no problem accommodating one person. After all, he could be the one to prove himself."

Finally, Yusuf Khan was given a three-year contract, which was to be renewed every year with a salary of Rs 500 per month and annual increments of Rs 200. Once hired Devika Rani thought his name was too plain and so, the hunt for a suitable screen name began. Yusuf wanted to refuse but he was struck with the thought of his strict Pathan father who would not have liked him to join the profession of **bhaands**, which is how the film and theatrical career was looked upon by the conservatives of that era. Hiding behind a screen name was the ideal thing to do and so, he went along.

Pandit Narendra Sharma, then a writer with the studio, came up with three choices: Vasudev, Jehangir and Dilip Kumar. Yusuf himself liked the sound of Jehangir but the litterateur Bhagwati Charan Verma, who was also working with the studio as a story and scriptwriter and who knew that Devika Rani was secretly looking for a replacement for the departing Ashok Kumar, suggested Dilip Kumar. Devika Rani agreed and Dilip Kumar was born.

Life at Bombay Talkies wasn't easy but it was an institution where Dilip Kumar learned a lot about acting, films and even life itself! Discipline was strict and no one was excluded from it. A shabby dress or a flamboyant shirt could attract instant reprimand. Recalling the atmosphere of the studio several years later, Dilip said, "As a young actor attached to Bombay Talkies I found that I was required to read extensively from the institution's library which comprised 14,000 books. I had to conform to certain norms of dress and behaviour. Over and above this, we had the company of the best literary minds of that era. There were so many famous people taking to the cinema which was then in its formative years."

The younger actors were expected to attend the studio every day irrespective of whether they were required on the sets of not. The fine for any misdemeanour was a deduction of Rs 100 from the pay packet. One day Dilip Kumar decided to play hookey and watch a matinee at the Metro. During the interval he came out for a cup of tea and practically ran into Devika Rani who had come to see the film with Lady Enakshi Rama Rao (the actress-wife of filmmaker Mohan Bhavnani), Begum Jamshedji (wife of industrialist-hotelier J.R.D.Tata) and the entire Jeejeebhoy family. Dilip Kumar was aghast but Devika Rani coolly called out to him and introduced him around as "a conscientious young man". She also called out to her driver Laxman and told him, "**Saab ko studio chhod ke aao**." Dilip Kumar was lulled into believing that he had been forgiven but on the first of the next month he discovered that Rs 100 had been deducted from the salary.

During another instance Ashok Kumar ran out of cigarettes while on the sets and was desperately craving for a smoke. There was no way he could leave the studio to purchase a packet and no one else would volunteer to do it either. Ashok Kumar knew that Devika Rani had a packet of her own cigarettes in her office but he dare not remove one because he had already been caught doing that on several occasions. Eager to help his mentor, Dilip Kumar volunteered to help him. He slipped into Devika Rani's office and did bring back a cigarette. He was certain that no one had seen him "steal" the cigarette but Devika Rani had her set of informers for on the first of the next month his pay packet was short by Rs 100. The irony was that she not only knew who stole the cigarette but also knew for whom it was stolen!

Chapter Four

– *Learning the Ropes* –

May 1942. Bombay Talkies Studio, Malad, Bombay. He was a mere 19 years 5 months old and he had never acted in his life before, let alone faced the camera. In fact he was so painfully shy that he would often bunk lectures rather than face the girls in his class. But here he was playing the second lead opposite a new leading lady Mridula. The hero was the handsome Agha. The film was *Jwar Bhata* and the director was Amiya Chakraborty, who had begun at the studio as an extra in a couple of films and then worked his way up to the position of director. He had just finished directing a superhit film *Basant* which had catapulted him to the ranks of young directors to be looked out for.

Curiously enough one of Amiya Chakraborty's junior assistants was the eldest son of a noted star who wanted his son to start at the bottom. Dilip Kumar knew the boy well because not only had they played football together in college but their families had also known each since the Peshawar days. In fact, his father was a great friend of the boy's grandfather Lala Baseshwar Nath. The youngster was Raj Kapoor who not only wanted to act in films but also wanted to write, produce and direct them.

The very first shot required him to run so as to "rescue" the heroine. Having played football and hockey all his life, Dilip ran as fast as he could – hoping probably to convey the urgency that only a hero could feel while rescuing the heroine. But before he could reach Mridula, the director had called "Cut". "You are running much too fast. Our camera cannot follow you at that speed," said Chakraborty and back it was to running once again. Several takes later Dilip managed the gentle trot that the director wanted and the shot was okayed.

The actual rescue happened only the next day by which time Dilip's embarrassment had had ample time to rise to the fore. "I was too nervous to even touch her," he recalls, "let alone hold her with both hands." This was something his career as a sportsman had not prepared him for. And if there was anything which would have made him give up a career in films it would have been this.

Days later, when he had found his bearings at Bombay Talkies, Dilip Kumar confided to his older and much more experienced colleague Ashok Kumar, "I feel so nervous when I touch my heroine that my hands go cold." Ashok Kumar, who had also begun his career with a somewhat similar nervousness, replied, "Do one thing. Rub your hands hard just before the shot to warm them up! I always do it!"

Jwar Bhata took an unusualy long time to make and was eventually released in Bombay on November 29, 1944. The film opened to a lukewarm critical response and even the presence of Amiya Chakraborty as writer-director could not salvage the film which dealt with the age-old story of a girl (Mridula) torn between the love of two men (Agha and Dilip Kumar). Filmdom's leading journal *Film India* dismissed the film as "nothing outstanding" but was particularly savage in its criticism of Dilip Kumar: "Dilip Kumar, the new hero of Bombay Talkies, is an anaemic addition to our film artistes. He needs a lot of vitamins and a prolonged treatment of

Jwar Bhata

proteins before another picture can be risked with him. He looks gaunt and famished and strikes one as a long ill-treated convict who has escaped from a jail. His appearance on the screen creates both laughter and disappointment. His acting effort in this picture amounts to nil."

In spite of this harsh reaction Dilip Kumar seems to have garnered a certain amount of fame for the comedian Mukri remembers an incident, which occurred soon after the release of the film. Dilip Kumar and Mukri, who had made his acting debut a couple of years earlier with Zia Sarhady's *Nadaan*, were travelling by train. Those were the days when everyone from the producers to the stars to the general staff took the train while travelling to the far off suburbs of Malad (where Bombay Talkies was situated) or Goregaon (where Filmistan was based).

Two European girls got into the compartment and immediately recognised Dilip Kumar. One of the girls went up to Mukri and whispered into his ears, "Is this the film star Dilip Kumar?" Not to be outdone Mukri whispered back, "Yes! That is Dilip Kumar." This whispering angered Dilip Kumar, who, after the girls had got down, gave Mukri a dressing down pointing out the importance of "sober, responsible and serene behaviour".

Soon after Mukri and Dilip Kumar found themselves working on yet another Bombay Talkies film, *Pratima*, being directed by noted actor Jairaj. This time they were sharing a make-up room. Though they had known each other since their college days they were not really very close but this gave them the opportunity to get to know each other. Mukri laughs, "Dilip was always a very reserved person and very particular about the way he carried himself. Unlike him, however, I was a notorious person. Whenever he disapproved of my mischief, he would throw my things out of the make-up room." In spite of these displays of temper, they grew close to one another and Mukri became almost a permanent fixture in the later-day Dilip Kumar films.

Jairaj, who had wangled an assignment as director from Devika Rani, was an actor who had made his debut in the fading years of silent cinema. He was keen on making a film on Leo Tolstoy's literary classic *Resurrection* but Bhagwati Charan Verma and Narendra Sharma, the two famous litterateurs then working with Bombay Talkies, suggested a reworking of Munshi Premchand's *Godaan*. But M.I.Dharamsey, who was designated Producer for the project, preferred to make *Pratima*, an original script written by Bhagwati Charan Verma. And so, it was decided to make *Pratima*. Dilip Kumar was selected to play the lead opposite the more established Swarnalata.

Pratima was completed much faster than *Jwar Bhata* but met with more or less the same fate as Dilip Kumar's first starrer. This time there was nothing to salvage the film. Jairaj was not a big-time director and nor was Swarnalata a very big star. *Film India* called it "a chain of still photographs stuck together for film purposes". The magazine was even more savage on Dilip Kumar: "Dilip Kumar seems to have gone more anaemic since his last picture. He now presents a hollow chest, limp arms, shaky legs and a woe-begone look, suggesting an illness of several years. When a man with these looks plays the hero it must be the end of motion picture glamour. Dilip Kumar does not act at all and we doubt whether he will ever act in future."

But act he did ... and in the very next film. Dilip Kumar, it would seem, was waiting for a mentor who would guide him through the intricacies of film histrionics. Devika Rani had left Bombay Talkies after her marriage to the Russian-born painter Svetaslov Roerich and made her home in Bangalore. Bombay Talkies had now been taken over by Shiraz Ali Hakim, builder of the Famous Cine Laboratories and Studios at Mahalaxmi in Mumbai. Hiten Chowdhury, who had provided so much moral support while recruiting Dilip Kumar in 1942, had been brought in as Controller of Productions, which made him the virtual boss of the day-to-day running of the studio. He invited the famed cinematographer and director of New Theatres, Nitin Bose, to make a film for the company which had suffered a series of flops which had harmed both its reputation and coffers. Nitin Bose had been given a free hand to make the film and the subject he had chosen was Rabindranath Tagore's famous story *Naukadubi* (*The Wreck*) written in 1906.

Meera Mishra, one of Dilip's leading ladies in *Milan*

The film was to be made in two versions: the Bengali version was to retain the original title while the Hindi version was to be rechristened *Milan*. The paperwork was ready and all that was left was to select the cast. Nitin Bose had brought along a popular Bengali actor Abhi Bhattacharya to play the lead opposite Meera Mishra and Mira Sarkar. Once on the sets, however, it became apparent that Abhi's Hindi diction was not good enough for him to play the lead in the Hindi version. Hiten Chowdhury suggested the name of Dilip Kumar but Nitin Bose was skeptical. After all, the actor's first two films had not garnered any credits. However, after the very first rehearsal Nitinda okayed Dilip Kumar's choice. The Marathi actress Ranjana was brought in to play Mira Sarkar's role in Hindi. Radhu Karmakar, who later became Raj Kapoor's permanent cameraman, made his debut as cinematographer with this film.

Unknown to everyone Dilip Kumar had spent the last few years honing his craft as an actor. He had always been a fan of Hollywood films but now, he had begun to watch them closely. He saw them again and again so as to imbibe the naturalness of their actors like Paul Muni, Spencer Tracy, Henry Fonda, James Stewart, John Gielgud, Ingrid Bergman, Vivien Leigh and Lana Turner. Many years later he recalled, "James Stewart and Henry Fonda, I found, could bring their faces and voices to convey two entirely different expressions at the same time, something like contra-melody. From Paul Muni I came to absorb the art of character delineation. I couldn't believe he could achieve the variations that he did playing Louis Pasteur on the one hand and a fugitive from a chain gang on the other."

Nitin Bose, already a formidable name in Indian cinema, instinctively understood what Dilip Kumar was aiming at and instantly took the young lad under his tutelage. For the first time since he had joined the trade, Dilip Kumar met a master who had the same aspirations as he had: to shun all artifice. "It was absolutely essential, Nitin Bose said, for me to concentrate single-mindedly on their performances to be able to assess them in depth and glean, from their art, worthwhile lessons for my advance as an artiste. It was this insight on how to draw the most out of watching great artistes perform that made me realise what it took to become a real actor."

Both versions of the film progressed smoothly and though Nitin Bose had to shuttle between Bombay and Calcutta towards the end of its production because he was supervising the scripting of his next venture (*Drishtidaan*), *Milan* turned out quite well. *Milan* was not a huge success but it did fare better than the company's last two ventures. But once again *Film India* savaged the film calling it "lousy boring stuff". It added, "As to old Tagore, death has silenced his protest and knowing very well that dead men tell no tales, Nitin Bose can consider himself safe from reproach for wrecking *The Wreck* beyond all recognition."

Describing Dilip Kumar's choice as the leading man as "heart-rending", the reviewer once again emphasised: "The boy looks

Ranjana and Dilip Kumar in *Milan*

anaemic and though he seems to make an honest attempt to deliver the goods as an artiste, he sadly fails to convince. Dilip Kumar has come to the screen with an unfortunate face and no one is going to imagine a hero's portrait on the screen with that face."

During the making of *Milan*, producer-director Shaukar Hussein Rizvi had offered Dilip Kumar a single film contract. The film was *Jugnu* opposite the famed singer-actress Noorjehan. Hiten Chowdhary encouraged the young actor to accept the film since it would do him good to act in an "outside" film. In any case, Dilip Kumar's three-year contract with Bombay Talkies was coming to an end and with the completion of *Milan*, he would be free to work with any other company or even take up work on a freelance basis, which was fast becoming the fashion.

Around the time *Milan* and *Jugnu* were being made Dilip was also approached by a stunt filmmaker to play the lead in his film for a fairly large fee. Dilip was not too keen since action films were considered C-grade stuff and looked down upon by the mainstream industry but he also needed the money desperately. In fact, he had asked Hiten Chowdhary to advance him a loan to which Hitenda had readily agreed. When this offer was made Dilip asked Hitenda if it would be right for him to take up the assignment. Hiten argued that one action film would not really mar Dilip's career since he was being approached by other producers so he told Dilip that it was all right. But Dilip thought about it all night and came back to Hitenda asking for the loan since he had decided not to accept the film. Thus, even as a fledgling actor Dilip had the correct judgement.

Jugnu revolved around a group of college students led by Dilip Kumar (playing Suraj) who defy conventional norms and established authority. *Film India* trashed the film as "a dirty, disgusting, vulgar picture" but the reviewer had mellowed down enough to admit that "he (Dilip Kumar) tries to do his bit but he doesn't match well with Noorjehan. Dilip, however, speaks his dialogue well." The magazine

Noorjehan with Dilip Kumar in *Jugnu*...their only film together

led the insistent chorus seeking a ban on the film – going to the extent of sending an advance copy of the review to the then Home Minister of Bombay, Morarji Desai, who promptly banned the film in October 1948.

However, several months later saner counsel prevailed and the ban was lifted. The film's songs had already become a big hit with the audience and the film went on to become a much bigger hit – too late unfortunately to help anyone. By then Noorjehan had decided to migrate to the newly-created Pakistan, making *Jugnu* her first and last film with Dilip Kumar.

Chapter Five

– A Star in the Making –

1948 was a landmark year for Dilip Kumar. It was the first year of an intensely prolific period. In just 13 years (1948-1961) he was to act in as many as 31 films – a little more than half the films he made in his entire career which spans 47 years (1944-1991). His score card till then read: Four releases. Three flops. One controversial hit. The best review he had got was a lukewarm "he tries to do his bit" – not enough to base a career on! But Fate was to intervene and take an active part in his affairs very soon. Till then there were plenty of films which he had signed in the wake of *Jugnu*'s success.

Among the films that Dilip Kumar had signed in the wake of *Jugnu*'s success was a three-film deal with Filmistan, which had been established by Rai Bahadur Chunilal and Sashadhar Mukherji when they left the Bombay Talkies in 1942. Sashadhar Mukherji's brother-in-law and Dilip's friend and mentor at Bombay Talkies, Ashok Kumar, along with a few other Bombay Talkies colleagues were a part of Filmistan at Goregaon. Ashok Kumar, the first of Indian cinema's "natural" actors, was already a major star. Though past his prime he continued to be accepted in lead roles. Sashadhar Mukherji, designated Controller of Productions, was a big-name producer in his own right with a formidable list of "hits" to his credits. Both were cultured well-read men who had an uncommon common sense with an inherent intuition for what the audience wanted.

The first of the three Filmistan films to be released was also Dilip's first release of the year: *Shaheed*, described by its makers as "a romantic story with the background of the 1942 struggle". On its release, *Film India* queried, "good romantic melodrama but where is the 1942 movement?" In spite of that, *Shaheed*, written and directed by Ramesh Saigal, was actually the right film at the right time. Saigal himself had started as a clapper boy with Pancholi Art Productions in Lahore and worked his way to becoming an assistant director. He had turned up in Bombay after the Partition and co-authored (with Inder Raj Anand) the stageplay *Deewar* for Prithvi Theatres. *Shaheed* was only his second film but he was destined to become a major filmmaker in the 1950s.

Playing the female lead was the talented and beautiful newcomer Kamini Kaushal, who had made her debut a year earlier with Chetan Anand's *Neecha Nagar*, the first Indian film to bag a major award at the Cannes Film Festival. Born into a highly educated, cultured and wealthy family, Uma Sood (nee Kashyap), had been a brilliant student of Lady MacLagen School and the Emily Kinnaird College in Lahore. She stood first in the Matriculation and third in the Bachelor of Arts examinations. She was also an active member of the Dramatic Societies of her school and college and was a popular radio artiste in Lahore. Dilip Kumar, in spite of his shy manner and tousled hair (or maybe because of it!) was as handsome and as charming as they came. Both stars were comparatively new – having done only a few films before coming to *Shaheed* – and yet, they had individual reputations to consolidate. On-screen they were perfectly matched.

Off-the-screen, the two young people fell totally and hopelessly in love. Totally, because they had eyes for no one else. Hopelessly, because Kamini Kaushal was married – even if it was to the husband of her elder sister whom she had adored and who had died of tuberculosis. She was the daughter of a renowned botanist S.R.Kashyap – a President of the Indian Science Congress and Dean of the Punjab University before the Partition – the sister of a military officer and now the wife of a high-ranking Port Trust official B.S.Sood. More than that, she had two step-daughters for whose security and future she had married in the first place. All that was now at risk! But the heart has its own reason and reasoning. Maybe they just could not help it!

Kamini Kaushal...perfectly matched

Apart from the on-and-off-screen chemistry between Dilip Kumar and Kamini Kaushal, the highlight of the film was the confrontation scenes between Dilip Kumar and his screen father, Chandramohan, an exceedingly handsome green-eyed actor with a formidable histrionic reputation who had once claimed that if he left his coat on the sets it would also "act". That alone must have been a great incentive for an actor who was primed to give off his best, an actor who was keen to improve himself with every film that he did and thus change the very nature of Indian film histrionics.

This time *Film India* was more fulsome in its praise for Dilip's performance. "So far as acting is concerned," it said, "Dilip steals the picture with its deeply felt and yet perfectly natural delineation of the main role. Sensitivity and understatement are the outstanding characterestics of his acting."

Expectedly, the film was a sensational hit. The film's intensely patriotic theme, coming in the wake of the country's independence and the resulting euphoria, was one of the major causes of the film's success. Dilip's scenes with Chandramohan were the talk of the town. When Chandramohan as Rai Bahadur enters the courtroom to defend his rebel son, publicly renouncing his British embellishments, there were cheers from the crowd. Equally popular were the love scenes with Kamini Kaushal. *Film India* hinted at what was actually happening behind-the-scenes with, "The two of them act some of the tenderest, most intimate and most moving love scenes that have ever been seen on the Indian screen."

The only tragedy that marred the happiness of meeting Kamini and being part of a film which was bound to give him a firm place in

Mela

the Indian film industry was the death of his beloved mother Ayesha Begum on August 27, 1948 when Shaheed was still being shot. Two years later, on March 5, 1950, her husband Sarwar Khan was destined to follow her. Both were buried at Deolali. Thus both his parents never witnessed the heights which Dilip Kumar eventually attained. Dilip's eldest sister Sakina (fondly known as Apaji) became a "mother" to the family.

Dilip followed up the success of *Shaheed* with another big hit of the year – Wadia Movietone's *Mela* – this time opposite Nargis, who was, by then, a big star. How *Mela* came about in those volatile post-Partition days is a story in itself. Music director Naushad and director S.U.Sunny were staying with J.B.H.Wadia at his palatial bungalow at the Worli Sea Face for additional safety. Mrs Hilla Wadia suggested that J.B.H. make a film with Naushad, who was already a major star on the musical horizon. Naushad was willing but suggested S.U.Sunny's name as director. Strangely enough it was also decided to credit Sunny as the producer of the film. (Or maybe Sunny was the actual producer and just wanted the Wadia umbrella to tide over the post-Partition anger against Muslims in general.) S.U.Sunny, in turn, brought in story-writer Azm Bazidpuri, who would write many of Dilip starrers in the 1950s.

With the basic elements of the film in place, Nargis was signed to play the leading role and the search for a fresh-looking young man began. The search ended with Dilip Kumar and *Mela* went into production. Years later Dilip Kumar recalled how he had signed up for Mela, "Since the hero was the last to be signed all other aspects of the film had been finalised – particularly the music. Sunny did not tell me anything about the film but just played one song for me: the Mukesh-Shamshad **mera dil todne wale**. I was hooked. I did the unthinkable: I signed the film because I just fell in love with that one song. I have never done such a thing again." Dilip Kumar's faith in the music and Naushad, Sunny and Wadia's faith in the actor were vindicated.

Kamini Kaushal with co-actors in *Nadiya Ke Paar*

Since the majority of the crew was Muslim it was thought advisable not to shoot at Wadia's studio (now the Rajkamal Studios) in Parel. The unit was therefore shifted to the Famous Cine Laboratories and Studios, now taken over by Jagmohan Rungta. *Mela* and its music went on to become the biggest hit of the year but that still did not stop *Film India* from calling it "far from being sensible; it is at once stupid and reactionary." The magazine tried to have the film recalled but no one was listening. On the contrary, the film proved to be a golden jubilee hit and was shown to Queen Elizabeth II on her yacht Britannia during her visit to Southeast Asia in 1954.

Not only did *Mela* establish Dilip Kumar as a major star in the making, it brought together Naushad, Sunny and Dilip Kumar who would together make many more films. It brought Azm Bazidpuri to the fore as a story and dialogue writer and he would write many a Dilip Kumar hit in the years to come. It also brought together the Nargis and Dilip Kumar pair, which would, without being romantically paired in real life, act together in six more films. It would also give Dilip Kumar his greatest hit of that period because Naushad would recommend him as the third angle of the *Andaz* triangle to a once-reluctant Mehboob Khan.

With one hit under their belts, Naushad and the slightly junior Dilip Kumar became good friends and Naushad began visiting the Khan household. Naushad further endeared himself to the Khan family when he announced to Dilip's father, Ghulam Sarwar Khan, that he was a disciple of his old friend from Peshawar, Ustad Jhande Khan. Poor Ghulam Sarwar had by now reconciled to the fact that two of his sons had joined the world of **bhaands** but associations such as these must surely have brought joy to his heart that not everyone in films was "bad".

Another eminent personality who put in a good word for the young Dilip was none other than Maulana Azad. Recalls Dilip today, "He was annoyed when I got into films. But then he heard other people whom he respected relishing the idea. Once Maulana Azad, whom everyone revered, heard my father commenting caustically on my moving into films. Maulana Saab intervened on my behalf and said there's no telling what the future held for anyone. He also told my father to be proud of my achievements and implored him to be patient with my aspirations."

The year ended with the release of the second Filmistan film, *Nadiya Ke Paar*, directed by Kishore Sahu, who was a more than competent actor (having made his debut as an actor opposite none other than Devika Rani in *Jeevan Prabhat* in 1937), a prolific writer of short stories and a technically polished director (this being his seventh film). *Nadiya Ke Paar* is a tale of simple village lovers who meet, fall in love, only to meet a tragic end in the village river. This is the first time that Dilip Kumar actually dies at the end of the film, thus adding to his star lustre and mystery.

Film India gave its approval to this "technically attractive picture". While congratulating Kamini Kaushal for a "sparkling performance"

Dixit, Manorama, Gulab, Dilip Kumar and Gope in *Ghar Ki Izzat*

it did an about-turn on Dilip Kumar noting, "Dilip Kumar, who plays the hero, gives his stereotyped performance and becomes boring, being seen in too many pictures recently. The boy has no new tricks left, it seems." Reviews notwithstanding, the film was an instant hit with college students who could empathise with the chemistry of forbidden love. Kamini Kaushal and Dilip Kumar became the new screen lovers. The fact that they were madly in love off-the-screen only added to the mystique.

Three hits from three releases was a terrific hit rate. Dilip Kumar was going places but he was equally destined to take another step backward. That seemed to be the pattern that Dilip Kumar was falling into. The year 1949 dawned with an inconsequntial release for the young upwardly mobile actor: Ram Daryani's *Ghar Ki Izzat*. Worse, he hardly had a role in this highly improbable family melodrama which pits the uneducated mother-in-law (Gulab) against the educated daughter-in-law (Mumtaz Shanti) with the poor hero escaping the two by taking to drink.

Film India described the film as "trash supreme" adding that it was "another of those idiotic stories with reactionary content". Veteran actress Mumtaz Shanti with *Kismet*'s success halo still around her head gave her "usual good performance" but the story and direction was so lacklustre that the film sank without a trace and not even Manorama's and Gope's antics as the husband-and-wife insurance agents could see it through. About Dilip Kumar the magazine said: "With his thick eyebrows and overgrown top, Dilip Kumar looks like a little bear escaped from the zoo. He has given the same stereotyped performance as usual."

The other inconsequential release of the year was *Anokha Pyar* though it starred him opposite two well-known heroines: Nargis and Nalini Jaywant. The film was directed by his former Bombay Talkies colleague M.I.Dharamsey from a story and screenplay by Zia Sarhady who was to become a director of some note in the early 1950s with films like *Footpath* and *Humlog* before migrating to Pakistan and then to London. There was nothing unusual about the story which depicted the usual triangular romance without even an iota of novelty: a struggling writer falls in love with a society girl but is, in turn, loved by a poor flower seller.

He would act in only two films opposite Nalini Jayawant but years later he remembered her as "the best actress I have worked with". He adds, "She'd be punctuality personified, she'd bring an extra warmth to her performance, she'd be quite extraordinary even in her first

Kamini Kaushal and Dilip Kumar in *Shabnam*

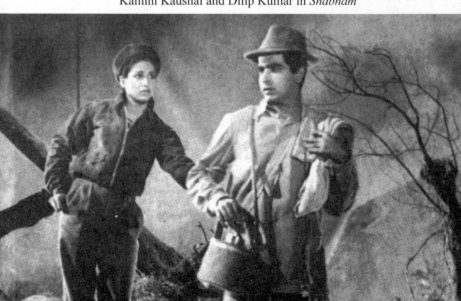

rehearsal." This was also Dilip Kumar's first film opposite Nargis after the success of *Mela* but they could not re-create the *Mela* magic. On the contrary there was a snide remark from *Film India*: "Dilip Kumar could have given a better performance but he seems to have missed his favourite heroine Kamini Kaushal." The other highlight was Anil Biswas's haunting music which was given voice by Mukesh who was to sing some more unforgettable songs for Dilip Kumar.

Described as "a thrilling tale of sighs and smiles", *Shabnam* was the last of the three Filmistan films Dilip had signed up for. Once again he was starred opposite Kamini Kaushal, which alone ensured that the film was a superhit. The off-screen romance was still very much on and that added to the attraction of the film. As *Film India* commented in its review: "Their love scenes give glimpses of realism and both the artistes seem to enjoy their romantic sequences."

At one point in the film when Kamini Kaushal dresses up as a boy Dilip Kumar looks deeply into her eyes and says, ""Tagore ne kaha tha: 'Tumhari aankhain do neeli jheelain hain aur mein un mein doob, doob jana chahata hoon." Whether Tagore ever said such a thing in his extensive writings is not known but the dialogue was quoted by young men all over India and in Pakistan and formed the template for future romantic dialogues.

Directed by Bibhuti Mitra, the film was set against the backdrop of the Japanese occupation of Burma but, contrary to its grim backdrop, it was an entertainer with a vengeance – with no less than "eleven songs and goodness knows how many dances". This was the formula which would be evolved into a fine art by the so-called "Sashadhar Mukherji school of filmmaking" (Subodh Mukherji and Nasir Hussain being its later-day proponents) in the 1950s and this would be the formula which Hindi cinema would use quite extensively in the decades to come. At that time, however, it was a novelty and fans crowded the theatres wherever the film was released. The film did not much add to Dilip Kumar's prestige as an actor but was undoubtedly a feather in his cap. He was well on his way to stardom.

Chapter Six

– *The First Milestone* –

Andaz was released on March 21, 1949 at the Liberty in Bombay, and was an instant box-office hit... and now, it is listed among Indian cinema's all-time hits.

Andaz is the first major milestone in Dilip Kumar's career. He had given good performances before *Andaz* ... he had had hits before *Andaz* ... but none gave him the star status that *Andaz* did. And more than that! The film established him as a major histrionic talent. It was with this film that the sobriquet Tragedy King got attached to his name for the rest of his career. In brief, there was no looking back after *Andaz*!

For Mehboob Khan, *Andaz* was a turning point in his career. Mehboob's films preceding *Andaz* were unadulterated romantic musicals with a quaint old-fashioned look (*Anokhi Ada*, *Anmol Ghadi*) and though they were huge commercial successes, Mehboob was keen on giving all his future films a modern look. Maybe it had something to do with the nation's upbeat mood in the immediate post-Independence period. Or maybe it had something to do with Mehboob's recent Hollywood visit where no less a filmmaker than Cecil deMille, who was also his idol, had described his early *Humayun* as "one of the finest examples of cinema art to come out of India".

The film industry in India was already in a state of flux. Old stars were on their way out and new faces were showing up in the trade papers every day. New stories were being told using the latest narrative techniques. Mehboob's script was ready and he wanted to make it in the best traditions of Hollywood. *Andaz* tells the story (by Shums Lakhnavi) of an immensely rich girl Neena (Nargis) who lives

With Nargis in *Andaz*

the life of the idle rich. She befriends Dilip (Dilip Kumar) who saves her from a riding accident. Dilip misunderstands her friendship and falls passionately in love with her. This misunderstanding is further fanned when Neena asks Dilip to look after her estates after the death of her father.

Enter Rajen, a childhood turned England-returned fiance who matches her step for step in her idle but larger-than-life lifestyle. In spite of the number of intense numbers Dilip croons to her, neither she nor Rajen realise he is putting into song his heartbroken torment. They continue to plan their wedding and it is only on the wedding night that Dilip reveals his love for Neena, thus sowing a suspicion in Rajen's mind that the two have had an affair. Matters come to a head and Neena shoots down Dilip. Neena is brought to trial but Rajen refuses to help her in her case until he discovers a crucial letter written by Dilip but never read. By then it is too late!

It is a trite story but the script (by S.Ali Raza) gives it a totally new dimension, imbuing it with so many unspoken insights into the idiosyncrancies of the rich, the nature of youthful bonding and the pangs of unrequited love. It is a dark moralistic tale of what happens when the permissiveness of a western lifestyle is allowed to impinge on what is considered to be Indian culture. In a sense Mehboob was merely echoing the doubts of a million parents who were apprehensive about the fate of their offsprings who had taken to an excessively western lifestyle in the immediate post-Independent era.

Ironically, the film itself is replete with the symbols of a westernised lifestyle: ballroom dancing and badminton games at the club; elaborate birthday parties with songs sung at the piano; the formal western dresses for both the sexes; the free inter-mixing of the sexes. It is as if the film advocates the very lifestyle it seeks to condemn. Mehboob also uses symbolism and metaphor in the telling of the story: the two male leads tossing a flower at each other as they verbally duel over their lady love (almost like a badminton match); Dilip appearing in

Neena's mirror almost as a physical representation of her innermost feelings for him.

Other highlights of the film include its low-key high-contrast cinematography (Faredoon Irani), the opulent sets (Keshav Mistry) and Naushad's eternally pleasant music. The songs are as fresh as they were way back in 1949. The musical highlight of the film is Mukesh breaking out of the Saigal mould and really coming into his own as well as Lata Mangeshkar singing for Nargis.

Mehboob Khan wanted fresh faces but not inexperienced newcomers. He signed Nargis because he had introduced her in *Taqdeer* and she was now a successful star. Nargis suggested Raj Kapoor with whom she was starring in *Aag*. Dilip Kumar was recommended by Naushad who had been favourably impressed with him while working in *Mela*. Unfortunately, Mehboob Khan was one of the film persons who had reacted adversely to the inclusion of Dilip Kumar in the cast of *Milan*. He had even confided to Hiten Chowdhary, "You have got a chance to make a film on your own but I cannot understand why you should take a risk with that new hero of yours."

That was in 1945. In 1948, however, Naushad's recommendation backed by the success of *Mela* and *Shaheed* was enough to get the role for Dilip Kumar. This time, however, Mehboob's permanent cameraman Faredoon Irani was not too happy with the choice. "Who is this monkey?" Faredoon is supposed to have asked Mehboob when the young actor came in on the first day for the shooting. Dilip went on to do many more films for Mehboob but he never really got along with Faredoon who continued with his dislike for the actor.

But Dilip vindicated his selection as one of the leading stars of *Andaz*. Calling it "Dilip Kumar's greatest performance so far", *Film India* said, "Dilip Kumar improves beyond recognition under Mehboob's direction. He casts off his usual mannerisms and becomes versatile in the role of Dilip, the frustrated lover. The way he portrays

The trio that set the industry
aflame...Raj Kapoor, Nargis
and Dilip Kumar

his struggle of suppressed emotions is a fine piece of histrionic art. This is easily Dilip Kumar's greatest performance so far."

Andaz collected a whopping seven lakhs in 28 weeks at the Liberty in Bombay, which had been inaugurated with the film. The film went on to become a classic but at the time of its run at the theatre the film was an ill omen for Mehboob and his stars. *Film India* in its December 1949 issue notes:

- Mehboob's mother passed away a week before the film's intended premiere which had to be delayed.

- Mehboob's younger brother died in a motorcycle accident.

- Mehboob's property at Bandra (which now houses Mehboob Studios) was attached under the Evacuee Ordinance and Mehboob was declared an evacuee.

- Nargis lost her mother because of a heart attack.

- Dilip Kumar was assaulted by **goondas** at Worli.

A rather telling epilogue for a future film classic.

Chapter Seven

– *Crafting the Image* –

Andaz became a milestone in the history of Indian cinema and in the process, made major stars out of Nargis, Raj Kapoor and, of course, Dilip Kumar. It would now become a problem for Dilip to live up to that image. In fact, his very next film gave evidence of the fact that not every film could add to his star value. *Aarzoo* was a film which lacked nothing. It was produced by Hiten Chowdhary and directed by Shahid Lateef. The film, based on Lateef's wife Ismat Chughtai's story, is lost in the pages of history.

If *Aarzoo* is at all remembered today it is because it further consolidated Dilip's image as the tormented lover who loses his sweetheart to the onslaughts of social propriety. It was the first of the films based on the Emily Bronte classic *Wuthering Heights* with Dilip Kumar playing the role of Heathcliffe, the orphan who is brought up by a wealthy landlord and grows up to be hated and terrorised by the landlord's son but loved by his daughter. The story had been suggested to Ismat as possible adaptation material by Dilip Kumar who was a great reader of classics.

Behind the scenes, however, another classic story was unfolding. Hiten Chowdhary had signed Kamini Kaushal to play the lead but had warned both Shahid Lateef and Ismat Chughtai not to reveal that Dilip Kumar had been signed for the film. The Dilip Kumar-Kamini Kaushal affair, three films old, was very much in the air but there was no saying what would happen if they fell out. Kamini, after all, was a married woman and though her husband Mr B.S.Sood was a tolerant man he could not have been unaware of what the film world was talking about. "Producers were afraid to sign Dilip Kumar and Kamini Kaushal because they were not sure when the affair would cool down and thus bring the film to an end," remembers Ismat.

Aarzoo

Both Ismat and Shahid were working with the acute understanding that *Aarzoo* would be the last film of the pair. One day on location, under the shade of a huge banyan tree, Ismat recalls having a long conversation with Kamini regarding her relationship with Dilip Kumar. She was all set to give up her family life and marry Dilip. Ismat dissuaded her from any such drastic step explaining the social consequences of her act. Kamini seemed disappointed since Ismat was generally seen as a social rebel because of her bold short stories and she had thought at least moral support for her cause would be forthcoming from that quarter.

One day when the film was reaching its conclusion and a few intimate scenes were to be picturised, Kamini turned up with her mother and brother. Her brother was in full military uniform with a pistol attached to his belt. There was no doubt that they meant business. Dilip himself was not a stranger to guns. Rumour has it that the husband of his first heroine Mridula (*Jwar Bhata*) had also turned up on the sets when he heard of the new hero's budding romance with his wife. It was further rumoured that Dilip hid in the ladies cloakroom to escape his wrath.

Andaz

This time apparently the hint was enough. Besides, Kamini herself had stopped responding. *Aarzoo* was released and did a reasonably good business. *Film India* condemned Ismat Chugtai's defiance of the spiritual sanctity of the Hindu marriage". The review adds, "It is this disgusting aspect of *Aarzoo* that has made the picture unpopular and caused it to fail at the box-offices. The direction of Shahid Lateef is amateurish." The fact that the affair was at an end is reflected in the attitudes of the artistes: "From the players, Kamini Kaushal, who plays the heroine does the bubbling sequences very well. Her reflective work, however, fails to be impressive. Dilip Kumar plays Badal very indifferently. He seems miles away from this situation even though Kamini sits so near him."

Dilip Kumar and Kamini Kaushal never worked together again and their oeuvre of four films is all that is left of their togetherness. Film history has added a small footnote to the Dilip Kumar-Kamini Kaushal romance, which is said to have inspired the 1960s' gem *Gumrah*, produced and directed by B.R.Chopra. Chopra, it seems, even wanted Dilip Kumar to play the lover but the actor refused saying, "The lover in the film is shown as a flippant character." The film was eventually made with Sunil Dutt, Mala Sinha and Ashok Kumar and is now one of the all-time hits of Hindi cinema.

Things were quiet on the personal front because his next four films were with Nargis, who, in a sense, was already emotionally and professionally committed to the R.K.Films banner. But this did not mean that Dilip Kumar the actor was quiet on the professional front. The recent heartbreak must have fuelled the roles that he was then playing in the wake of *Andaz*'s success. The huge success of *Mela* had not been forgotten and the main players in that film – Naushad, S.U.Sunny and Azm Bazidpuri – had come up with another tale: *Babul*, about a village postmaster who is caught up in the love of two girls, the rich town girl whom he loves and the other who cooks and keeps house for him and is in love with him.

'riangular romances would never be the same again...Nargis, Raj Kapoor and Dilip Kumar

Dilip Kumar was signed to play the role of the spineless postmaster whose life ends in tragedy because he is unable to articulate his choice very clearly. The film was another big hit and *Film India* praised Dilip Kumar for striding through the picture "with a pathetic poverty of a licked spineless lover who has neither the courage to love nor the guts to ask and take what he wants. It is great work and the ease with which Dilip Kumar portrays the role makes one wonder whether the man himself has lived through similar moments of pathos and frustrations in his private life."

Chandulal Shah wanted to sign Dilip Kumar for an unusual story he had in his mind: a dissolute man, an atheist, extremely fond of

Babul

music, visits the notorious houses of dancing girls so as to savour the music. Once, while visiting his village, he hears a **bhajan** being sung by a **jogan** in a temple. Mesmerised, he waits outside the temple till she catches sight of him. She asks him not to come there ever again but he returns the next day and all the other following days ...

It was a captivating story and just right for Dilip Kumar's current image but the problem was that Dilip Kumar was playing the usual hide-and-seek with him. When Mehboob got to hear of it, he scolded Dilip, "Chandulal Shah is a veteran filmmaker. Refuse his film if you don't want to do it but at least go and meet him." Dilip went and met Chandulal Shah and even agreed to do the film. A grateful Shah rang up Mehboob to thank him. "How much did you sign him for," asked Mehboob. "For Rs 40,000," said Shah. To which Mehboob replied, "Did you know that his current price is Rs 60,000?" Chandulal Shah did not say anything but at the next Id he called Dilip, embraced him and gave him a packet containing Rs 20,000.

If Chandulal Shah had trouble signing the leading man he had even more trouble getting a director for the film. It was rejected by both Mahesh Kaul and Nitin Bose as "too risky". Eventually Kidar Sharma offered to make it and Chandulal Shah agreed provided he could make it within a month since he had resources only for a month's shooting. The film *Jogan* (originally titled *Sadhvi*) turned out to be a superhit and is today considered to be one of the classics of Hindi cinema.

Nargis was the bone of contention between Dilip Kumar and Ashok Kumar in a film directed by Dilip's one-time mentor Nitin

Bose, *Deedar*. The film's story (once again written by Azm Bazidpuri) had shades of *Anmol Ghadi*: childhood sweethearts are parted because of their difference in status only to meet as adults. Blinded by a freak accident, Shyam (Dilip Kumar) spends his childhood and youth pining for Mala (Nargis), who is by then betrothed to Dr Kishore (Ashok Kumar), an ophthalmic surgeon. In the meantime the daughter of the family, which has adopted him, Champa (Nimmi), has been in love with him since their childhood.

The story is actually very simple but the complications of the love triangle create the dynamics of the script, which was a novelty then. Knowing that he would have to play a blind man in the film, Dilip asked Ashok Kumar, "How should I play a blind man?" His instant response was, "Close your eyes and you will not be able to see anything." To which Dilip retorted, "But I have to keep my eyes open and with open eyes I can see everything." Finally Ashok Kumar advised, "Go to Mahalaxmi and where the bridge ends you will see a blind beggar who begs with his eyes open. Observe him carefully." And Dilip actually drove down to Mahalaxmi to observe the beggar in action. A case of art imitating life!! Recalls Dilip today, "I spent quite a few days with him to get an insight into the world within him. He was very pleasant and would laugh at the darkness inside him. From him, I learned to be cheerful and had that beatific smile on my face in *Deedar*. It would have been far too run-of-the-mill to play a blind man with my eyes closed. It would have been an easy way out."

Dilip Kumar and Ashok Kumar shared a mischievous relationship. Once during the shooting of *Deedar*, Dilip Kumar bit Ashok Kumar's hand because he landed him a few punches in his excitement on

Dilip Kumar and Nargis in *Jogan*

giving a good take. Ashok screamed at the top of his voice and drew director Nitin Bose's attention to the bite. Nitin Bose was shocked, "How could you bite a senior actor like that?" Dilip retorted, "Why did he punch me? Am I not younger to him?" Nitin Bose, at a loss for an answer, arranged for first aid. Having received his due bit of attention, Ashok Kumar sidled up to Dilip Kumar and gleefully whispered to him, **"Dekha kaisa hungama mucha diya? Kaisa position down kar diya! Ashok Kumar ko kaatata hai aur oopar se daantata hai!"**

But Dilip Kumar had problems about the manner in which the scenes were being shot. He looked upon *Deedar* as an important film and was quite upset about it. In his anger he visited Naushad who had a major hand in the film's story and its making and complained, "You did not tell me about the manner in which the scenes were to be picturised. It is an important film and I am disappointed." Naushad tried to console but he would not budge. But when the film was released and he saw the reactions of the audience to the scenes he had found improperly filmed he was magnanimous enough to tell Naushad, "I withdraw my words. You were right and I was wrong. I am sorry."

The incident clearly shows that Dilip Kumar, as early as 1951, had already begun to think about how films should be made and though he was neither experienced enough nor a big enough star to openly find fault with Nitin Bose and Ashok Kumar, he did want something done about what he considered wrong. This kind of an all-round interest in the film and not only his role would lead to what was later termed as "interference" in the director's work.

As was expected the film was a hit. *Film India* called it "a beautiful picture with excellent production values". Praising Dilip's performance the review says, "It is a role natural to Dilip's tragic face. He lives it to perfection, every minute of it. And luckily he gets a playback singer who lends a rare thrill in the role with his soulful music. Whoever this singer is, his voice is a goldmine." The singer that *Film India* is talking about was Talat Mahmood, who came to be known as the voice of Dilip Kumar at least in the 1950s.

Hulchul was started at the same time as *Aarzoo* but it took two years in the making. Dilip Kumar was back to playing his favourite character in another rehash of *Wuthering Heights*. Directed by S.K.Ojha for producer K.Asif (who was then busy launching his magnum opus *Mughal-e-Azam* to give time to direct the film) and written by Hasrat, the film was described by *Film India* as "a touching tale of love told in songs and sighs and wound up in tragedy". Calling it a classic performance, *Film India* said this about Dilip Kumar, "He lives his role from scene to scene and attains frightening realism in the final climax." This was to be Dilip Kumar's last film with Nargis. Though there never was any romance, the relationship was a good one but it had soured due to misunderstandings.

The Kamini Kaushal romance had ended. His relationship with Nargis had soured. But there was another girl waiting in the wings. This time she took the initiative. On the sets of *Tarana* a romance was beginning to blossom. A single rose arrived in Dilip Kumar's make-up room on the first day. The bearer of the rose was the leading lady's personal make-up woman and companion. The message that accompanied the rose said, **"Agar aap mujhe chahate hain to yeh gulab kubool farmaiye, varna isse wapas kar dijiye."** The sender of the rose was the film's nubile heroine – just 17 years old but already a veteran of 30 odd films. She had very nearly become Dilip Kumar's first heroine in *Jwar Bhata* but for the fact that she had received Devika Rani's invitation to come down to Bombay from Delhi a little late and by the time she arrived, the film had already been cast. The young nubile heroine was Madhubala.

Unknown to Dilip Kumar a similar rose had been sent on the sets of another film to another handsome star, Premnath, with whom he would cross histrionic swords in *Aan,* and had been accepted with alacrity. Dilip Kumar fell for the ruse and the classically beautiful face behind it. The romance had begun. Even *Film India* was in its review of the film, "The teaming of Madhubala and Dilip Kumar for the first time on the screen had a lot to do with the degree of realism achieved in some of the romantic sequences which highlight the story."

Written by Dwarka Khosla (later to become a director in his own right), *Tarana* is a romantic tale punctuated with the usual villains and coincidences which prove the dictum that the path of true love never does run smooth – particularly when one of the lovers is Dilip Kumar. This story, fortunately and for a change, ends with the lovers united in the last frame. Packed with passionate love scenes the film (and obviously its new pair) caught the fancy of the audience which made the film a reasonable success. Madhubala made three more films with Dilip Kumar: *Sangdil, Amar* and the immortal *Mughal-e-Azam.*

Sangdil was based on another literary classic: Charlotte Bronte's *Jane Eyre.* Dilip Kumar plays the man tormented by a secret which he hides from the girl he loves (Madhubala). Eventually the secret is discovered: a deranged wife (Kuldeep Kaur) whom he has kept locked in an attic. It is a powerful Gothic tale, full of mystery and intrigue, but the film's director R.C.Talwar could not give it the mounting that the story deserved. Film India called it "a dull, boring and stupid picture". If the film is remembered today it is because of that one Talat song which he sang under Sajjad Hussein's baton: "**Yeh hawaa, yeh raat, yeh chandni ...**"

Their first film together...Madhubala and Dilip Kumar in *Tarana*

There was praise for Dilip Kumar, which had now become the norm, "Dilip Kumar puts to good use that famous face of his with its fixed tragic expression. He is quite faithful to the role and we certainly do not mind his whispers for a change in this loud industry." The last reference is to Dilip Kumar's whispered style of speaking his dialogues, which he had now adopted after being greatly impressed by Marlon Brando and his Method School of Acting – both of which had become the rage in Hollywood. In fact, like Marlon Brando in Hollywood, Dilip Kumar would snidely be referred to as The Great Mumbler by a few knowing journalists.

But *Hulchul, Tarana* and *Sangdil* were, for Dilip Kumar, comparatively inconsequential films. 1952 also witnessed the release of a film which was to become another all-time classic: *Daag*, directed by Amiya Chakraborty, his first director from the Bombay Talkies days. The film told the story of a compulsive alcoholic who is not above drinking away the money meant for his mother's medicine. The film is melodramatic but within its parameters Dilip Kumar gives a performance which underscores his torment at not being able to give up his addiction. He expresses his torment in a song which became exceptionally popular: **"Ai mere dil kahin aur chal ..."** The moral of the film: alcoholics can be reformed with love and understanding rather than ostracism. In many ways one can see shades of the *Devdas* which Dilip Kumar was to play a few years later.

Chapter Eight

– *Parting with Mehboob* –

It was the early 1950s. Colour had already arrived in Hollywood. Here in India, except for a few experiments in the early talkie era, no one had really made a film in colour. In fact, no colour processing laboratories existed in India then. The super success of *Andaz* had not left its maker behind. Mehboob was now not only one of the big producers of Bombay but the king of all that he could survey and obviously, in keeping with his status wanted to do something which no one was doing.

He wanted to make India's first colour film. And, as if this were not enough of a complication in his professional life, he wanted to make the film in 16 mm. and then get it blown up to 35 mm exhibition. The Technicolor Laboratories in London, with whom Mehboob and his cameraman Faredoon Irani were in close touch, suggested that they shoot the film in 16 mm Gevacolor and then have it blown up to 35 mm Technicolor.

The story of the film *Aan* was written by one-time writer-director of silent films, R.S.Choudhury and scripted by Agha Jani Kashmiri, Wajahat Mirza and Ali Raza. The film was to be the first film to be shot in Hindi, Tamil and English – though the English version was shelved later largely because the logistics were just not working out. Launched in 1949, the film was three years in the making and took 450 shooting days to make. But the effort was worth it because when released in India it was a smash hit.

Aan

This was the first time that Dilip Kumar was acting in a swashbuckling role complete with horse-riding and sword fights. The fans were thrilled. Their hero could do something more than weep over the girls he had lost. Nargis had been signed to play the lead and she even shot for a few days but her commitment to the R.K.Films banner (for

Nadira in *Aan*

which she was shooting *Awara*) compelled her to withdraw from *Aan*. An angry Mehboob vowed to create another Nargis – he had, after all, introduced Nargis with *Taqdeer* – and chose a Bombay-based Jewish girl to play the lead. Born Farhat Ezekiel, she was christened Nadira for the film.

Influenced by the larger-than-life films of producer Cecil DeMille, whom he had met on his first visit to Hollywood, Mehboob wanted to make a spectacular film which would take India and the world by storm. After all, hadn't his astrologer predicted exactly that? The film was released in London as *The Savage Princess* and in France as *Mangala, Fille des Indes*. Wherever it was released it attracted attention and the BBC even interviewed Dilip Kumar for one of their programmes. *Aan* put Indian cinema on the world map and showed the way for other Indian films to follow if they wanted success abroad. Not that many did!

Describing it as a cross between "Hollywood's fantasy adventures and imperial Roman spectacles", Philip Lutgendorf, Professor of Film at the University of Iowa, says about *Aan*, "Mehboob Khan went wild with the possibilities, crafting a highly surreal swashbuckler about a princely kingdom that lies, visually speaking, somewhere between Rajasthan and mad King Ludwig's Bavaria. Though there are echoes here and there of the real excesses and hybrid architectural fantasies of India's pre-independence maharajas, as well as themes glorifying peasant resistance and social egalitarianism, mostly this is an over-the-top operatic fairytale that looks, at times, like Disney animation come to life – though Disney would not have dared the out-front eroticism and fashion and footwear fetishism that permeates Mehboob's mise-en-scene."

Nailini Jaywant and Dilip Kumar in *Shikast*

While *Aan* was in the making Mehboob's second assistant Mehrish was hard at work on a story which he wanted to make as his debut film. The novel that had attracted his attention was Hall Caine's 1921 classic *Master of Man*, which told the story of a man who, in a moment of weakness, rapes an innocent village girl but does not have the guts to accept the repercussions of his act in public. Caught between his fiance and the girl he has raped he gives way and commits suicide. The novel was a powerful one and just the right subject for Mehboob's favourite star: Dilip Kumar. Ali Raza loved the subject and agreed to work on it. The proposed film was titled *Amar*.

While *Aan* was being released to world-wide acclaim, Dilip Kumar was busy completing two films which were to add to his oeuvre and enhance his status as an actor. *Aan* may have been welcomed by his fans as a change of pace and a reminder that he could play any kind

Dilip Kumar and Nimmi in *Amar*

of role but the tragic roles were the ones they preferred to see him in. *Shikast* tells the story of a man who returns to his village in the hope of selling his part of the property to his cousin but stays back when he realises that the village is being oppressed by him and his childhood sweetheart is a part of this exploitation. Though Ramesh Saigal had given Dilip Kumar a major hit in *Shaheed* he failed to replicate the success in *Shikast,* though the film is today considered to be miniature classic because of Dilip Kumar and Nalini Jaywant's sensitive performances.

Another Ramesh Saigal film, *Shikwah*, starring Dilip Kumar and Nutan, which was launched with great fanfare sometime in the early 1950s failed to reach fruition. A few songs composed by Anil Biswas were recorded for the film, in particular a Lata Mangeshkar and chorus song **raam kahaan ho aao**, written by Pandit Ramamoorty. A Talat song composed by Sajjad was also recorded for the film: **khushi dil ki barbadiyaan saath layee, mohabbat ki duniya basakar mitayee**. A few days shooting was also done before the film was shelved. A 1970s film *Film Hi Film*, based on scenes from incomplete films showed a few scenes from *Shikwah*. Dilip Kumar and Nutan were never paired again – probably because she formed a "hit" pair with brother Nasir Khan from *Nagina* in 1951 to *Aagosh* in 1953. The pairing was finally to take place nearly three decades later in Subhash Ghai's *Karma* (1986) and later *Kanoon Apna Apna* (1989).

The other film released in the same year (1953) was Zia Sarhady's *Footpath* in which he played a poor writer who is unwittingly sucked into a vortex of black marketers. Money begins to flow in with ease and he gets used to the good life till he is shaken out of his dreams of becoming a rich man quickly. Once again Dilip Kumar plays a character Noshu with various shades of grey – almost a negative role by Hindi film standards – and does so with great aplomb. An added attraction of the film is Meena Kumari, playing opposite him in a role which was not really long enough or meaty enough for an actress of her ability.

The film is a straightforward moralistic tale typical of the early post-independent era – particularly of Zia Sarhady whose other work includes *Aawaz* and *Humlog*, all three films being considered film classics of the Indian Left today. It is Dilip's underplayed performance, which prevents the film from becoming melodramatic or maudlin. The film has a wonderful scene which so epitomizes the character. Towards the end of the film the character wishes to give up his life of crime. The black marketers do not want to let go of him and warn him of dire consequences. "**Marwa do agar marwa sakte ho to**," he says laconically and walks down the staircase with a cigarette in the corner of the mouth. This is one of the rare films in which Dilip Kumar is shown smoking on the screen – but not the only one as claimed by his fans because he is also shown smoking in *Babul*.

By the time *Aan* was finished Mehboob had exhausted his money ... and probably himself. He had no fresh script in hand but it was necessary to start some film in order to keep the banner flying high. Ali Raza had finished working on the script of *Amar* but it had been promised to Mehrish. Mehboob was caught in a bind: could he really by-pass his first assistant (Chimankant Gandhi) and give a film to his second assistant? The script had turned out so well that for a moment even Dilip Kumar wanted to direct it. Eventually Mehboob diffused the impending crisis by opting to direct it himself. Mehrish was consoled with the direction of another film *Paisa Ya Pyar.*

The film went on the floors with Meena Kumari and Nimmi playing the two roles but within six days of shooting Meena Kumari was out

Babul

following a disagreement between Mehboob and Kamal Amrohi. Dilip saw this as a good chance to recommend his latest lady-love Madhubala for the film. Mehboob, eager to please his winning ace, agreed and the film went into shooting again. Dilip Kumar had by now become a major star. The inherent negativism of the character began to scare him. In order to keep his star image intact, he began to alter the script and eventually had a say in the making of the film.

The film opened to rave reviews but *Film India* summed up the crisis, "Dilip Kumar performs with his usual polish though his role cried for some cogent psychological development." However, the review lays the blame at the doorstep of the writers, "Mehboob needs better writers and a fully criticised scenario before he goes on the sets if he is not to repeat the attractive confusion that *Amar* is." The audience did not find it attractive and the film did not do too well at the box office. Writing several years later film critic Bikram Singh

Amar

gave *Amar* the place it deserved, "Today the film's teasing ambiguity looks much more acceptable. And the grey tones of the principal characters – defying the tradition of black and white characterisation – are something to marvel at."

Amar was to be Dilip Kumar's last film with Mehboob Khan. The parting of ways came about due to two misunderstandings. Soon after the making of *Amar,* Mehboob began to work on his magnum opus *Mother India*. Dilip was the automatic choice for the role of the bad son Birju. Dilip was now beginning to take more than a passing interest in the making of his films. He now wanted to be a part of the scripting process but Mehboob refused to alter his script to accommodate Dilip's deepest desire: to have the film revolve around himself. This hurt Dilip badly and he withdrew into a shell. But before that happened came another disappointment.

Dilip's younger brother Nasir Khan had made a visit to Pakistan in the immediate post-Partition period and had even stayed there long enough to star in the first truly Pakistani film but seeing no great prospects for himself had returned to India to discover that he had lost his market. Dilip was keen that he be given the lead in another film being made by Mehboob, *Aawaz* but the film's director Zia Sarhady was keen on signing up "fellow traveller" Zul Vellani. Not wanting to interfere in the creative decisions of a film he had already assigned to someone else, Mehboob told Dilip of his inability to do anything. Both these events took their toll and Dilip stayed away from future Mehboob productions – not that he had much of a role in either *Mother India* or *Son of India*, the two films Mehboob made before his death in 1964.

Chapter Nine

– *The Second Milestone* –

K.L.Saigal played it before him and Shahrukh Khan played it after him but mention *Devdas* and the only image that the mind's eye conjures up is that of Dilip Kumar, glass in hand, mouthing the immortal lines, "**Kaun kambakht bardaasht karne ke liye peeta**

The role that made him immortal...Dilip Kumar in *Devdas*

hai?" For Dilip, it was the culmination of a series of roles in which he played the weak-minded, spineless lover who refuses to fight back and prefers to die of heartbreak. It was also a character he found difficult to shed and ended up taking psychiatric help.

It was the first half of the 1950s and Bimal Roy was passing through a Saratchandra phase. He had made two Sarat stories into films in quick succession: *Parineeta* (1953) for Ashok Kumar and *Biraj Bahu* (1954) for Hiten Chowdhary. It was but natural for him to pick up *Devdas* as the concluding part of this informal trilogy particularly since he had been the cinematographer on the 1935 Barua version starring K.L.Saigal. Not only had the character fascinated him since he had first read the novel but he must have also developed definite ideas about how the novel was to be filmed. This was now his chance to show it.

By this time Dilip Kumar had played enough tragic lovers to be singled out as the first (and indeed, the only) choice. But the one person who was opposed to the idea was his previous producer Hiten Chowdhary, which was surprising because he had always been a Dilip Kumar sympathiser right from the days of *Milan*. The reason was different. Chowdhary felt that Dilip Kumar would prove expensive for Bimal Roy's conservative budget. After all, Dilip was a major star who charged in lakhs. To everyone's surprise Bimal Roy approached Dilip Kumar who promptly agreed – at Bimalda's price!

But if everyone agreed with the casting of Dilip Kumar in the title role there was considerable comment on the casting of the leading ladies. Nargis and Meena Kumari were considered and dropped and eventually the hugely talented Bengali actress Suchitra Sen, who was then just trying to make it in Hindi films, was selected for the role of Devdas's childhood sweetheart Parvati/Paro. Even more controversial was the casting of Vyjayanthimala in the complex role of the golden-hearted prostitute Chandramukhi. Probably her talents as a dancer were the reason for her being chosen but Bimal Roy consistently said

Suchitra Sen and Dilip Kumar in *Devdas*

that he also thought she would be an excellent actress though she had done nothing noteworthy in films till then.

Devdas was written in 1917 when Saratchandra himself was 17 years old and hence, the novel is sentimental and embarrassingly mushy. More than that it has its share of stereotypes which, according to film critic Sudhanva Deshpande, have since the filming of the novel become staples of Hindi cinema: "the hero unable to break the barriers of class and status to realise his love; the heroine, never unfaithful to her husband even though she cannot stop loving the hero; the golden-hearted prostitute and her unrequited love; the hero's suave, urbane friend".

Devdas and Paro are childhood friends who are highly individualistic and yet, cannot bear to be parted from one another. They grow up and it is suggested that he marry Paro but his father shouts down the proposal. The reason: Paro is from a lower caste and hence, unworthy of the family. Strangely enough he can accept her as his son's friend but not as his bride. Paro secretly visits Devdas and suggests that they elope but the vacillating lover turns her away.

Spurned by the man she loves, she agrees to be married to an old zamindar leaving Devdas to drown his sorrows in alcohol. He meets Chandramukhi who falls in love with him but he cannot offer her any hope in return. He is too wrapped up in his passion for Paro which takes him into a downward spiral to plumb the depths of alcoholic despair. Nothing can bring him solace. Eventually he makes that one final journey to Paro's doorstep ...

Bimal Roy thought that a Saratchandra story was "an asset". Talking about his Saratchandra phase, he said, "In every Sarat story there is good plot construction, convincing

Suchitra Sen and Dilip Kumar in *Devdas*

characterisation, truthful yet dramatic situations and telling dialogue, the sum total of which strikes a deep human note. These strong points are good material for the filmmaker." But Bimal Roy also saw a trap: "Let the filmmaker change a Sarat story and the critics will leap out of their skins. Let him adhere faithfully to the original and they will demand more detailed development."

It is probably because he had so much respect for the original material that the Bimal Roy version is considered to be the one closest to the novel. There are deviations to be sure but they are either cinematic improvisations or interpretations of the original text which are well within the rights of a sensitive filmmaker.

Dilip Kumar refused to see the original 1935 version starring Saigal before he embarked on playing the role, saying, "Frankly, when you remake something, it is better not to see too much of the original. At least then there is some contrast. A remake should never be made with the intention to better earlier versions; with that notion of superiority."

The film's writer Nabendu Ghosh remembers an incident that happened on the sets, "I remember, one day, we had a tea break. We found Dilip wandering alone, agitated. He seemed to be in deep thought and would not come near us. I went to him and asked, 'Yusufbhai, aap bahut pareshan lag rahe hain [You seem very troubled]?'

"He said, 'Nabhendubabu, woh teeno mere kaandhe pe baithe hue hain (Those three are weighing me down).'

"I asked, 'Kaun teen (Which three)?'
"He said, 'Saratbabu, Pramatesh Barua aur Kundan Lal Saigal.'."

Though he had played similar roles before, playing Devdas was tough on Dilip Kumar. He remembers, "I found it difficult to do Devdas during the first eight to ten days of shooting. I gradually drifted into it, bringing Devdas closer to my own personality. Often an actor has to divorce his personality from the character but that wouldn't have worked. No actor is bigger than the material he is essaying, he has to give it an interpretation from his own understanding of life, he has to blend his experiences with the alien's."

Devdas was released on March 30, 1956 at the Roxy cinema in Bombay and went on to become one of Indian cinema's enduring classics. *Film India* hailed it as "a picture of artistic grace and great appeal". Commenting on Dilip Kumar's performance *Film India* wrote, "Dilip Kumar plays the coveted but complex role of Devdas and he fits the role very well. This is the first time that Dilip has made an almost perfect attempt to merge himself into the role and at places it is extremely difficult to separate the two."

Chapter Ten

– Reworking the Image –

1956. Dilip Kumar had been playing tragic roles uninterrupted for more than a decade. As a film critic pointed out, "If rebellion became angst with Guru Dutt and grew romantic with Raj Kapoor, it was transmuted into inner torment with Dilip Kumar." And it was not merely a matter of playing such roles. Dilip Kumar was known to submerge his personality so completely in the creation of his character. As *Film India* had once commented while reviewing an earlier film *Deedar*, "This boy is easily our greatest tragedian of the screen – his forte being the portrayal of mental masochism under the stupor of frustrative love. His agony in such roles is so vivid and intense that he makes the people forget the actor and takes them to live with the character."

Something had to give way ... and it did! As Dilip Kumar himself confessed, "Yes, the Tragedy King. He was getting into the marrow of my bones and disturbing my personal peace. Because that's what I started believing, that I was born to suffer and to die."

He recalls those harrowing years: "I did face an acute personality problem, the problem of stardom, and of projecting myself into fictitious characters. I had to break my hostility towards them and still keep in touch with the larger reality. I referred this matter to drama coaches and psychiatrists who asked me to shift to comedy. I was with Dr. Woolf for about two to three years and with Dr. W. D. Nicol for about three years. King George VI as well as Sir Anthony Eden used to be his patients. He was a senior man and a very affectionate person. In India, I went through psychoanalysis under Dr Ramanlal Patel. I hadn't become a loony or anything. I just needed someone to talk to me. It gave me stability and poise."

Cutting through the jargon what all these drama coaches and psychiatric experts advised was that he should take up lighter roles ... roles which would not demand so much from his personality. He had played the swashbuckling hero before, with great success and popular acclaim in Mehboob's *Aan*. So why not play him again? The opportunity arose even as *Devdas* was being made. It came in the shape of a short stout South Indian named S.M.S.Naidu, owner of Pakshiraj Studios in Coimbatore.

Naidu had just made and released a colossal hit in Tamil called *Malai-k-Kalan*. Money was flowing in by the sackfuls. The sets of the film were still standing at his studio in Coimbatore. He was hit by a brainwave: why not make the film in Hindi? He came to Bombay with the idea of signing the biggest stars and remaking the film which, he was sure, would rake in twice the amount of money. He wanted the biggest star and who could be bigger than Dilip Kumar? The problem was: riding high on his success and rumoured to be obsessively choosy, Dilip took months to even say a "yes" to doing a film.

The Tragedy Queen meets the Tragedy King in a comedy...Meena Kumari and Dilip Kumar in *Azaad*

A showing of the Tamil version was arranged for Dilip Kumar and he was aghast with what he saw: it was a hardcore Robin Hood-kind of film packed with songs, dances, mystery, adventure, sword fights, opulent sets, disguises. Absolutely not the kind of film which Dilip Kumar would deign to act in – *Aan* notwithstanding. But Naidu was cocksure about what he had in his hands. He told Dilip, "Look! How many Dilip Kumars see a film? I made 25 lakhs on this film and I am sure I will make another 40 lakhs on the Hindi version."

Dilip tried refusing the film but Naidu just wouldn't let him get away with it. He followed him everywhere. Eventually Dilip gave in and signed on the dotted line, probably reminding himself that it was exactly what the doctor ordered in any case. Meena Kumari was also signed to play the leading lady. Both stars known for their intensely serious in-depth roles were signed for a swashbuckling adventure to be made deep in the South in just three months! Impossible! The film industry forgot about the film till come March 18, 1955 and all the roads in Bombay led to the Minerva theatre near Grant Road in Bombay.

Film India was almost admiring in its review, "*Azaad* is a picture planned for profits with a lethal vengeance of which only a cool and designing South Indian is capable." It was a film designed to please the crowds and it did just that in ample measure. It also made an enormous amount of money, just like the Tamil version. More than that, it gave concrete proof that both Dilip Kumar and Meena Kumari were adept at comedy. Curiously enough, it won for Dilip Kumar his second Filmfare award for Best Actor. What other films the "cool and designing South Indian" made after this one is not known but he never made a Hindi film again.

With *Azaad* began Dilip Kumar's association with the South Indian film industry, which had made its entry in the Hindi film market way back in the early 1950s. S.S. Vasan, widely known as the Showman of the South Indian film industry, had begun to make his presence on the all-India scene after he had been elected president of the Film Federation of India in 1955. Dilip Kumar, known for his close association with film industry causes, must have interacted with him and eventually agreed to do a film in the South. The South Indian film producers were known to be a disciplined lot and good paymasters. And his first experience had proved to be a good one.

A special highlight of Vasan's *Insaniyat* (1955) was that it co-starred Dilip Kumar with Dev Anand and Bina Rai. Dilip Kumar had the usual role of the man who loses his girl to another (Dev Anand) and is eventually blamed by her for sacrificing her husband's life because of his former love for her. There are several scenes between the two stars but there is no fire since Dev Anand is openly uncomfortable. Recalls Dev Anand, "My personality just didn't click with the character of the rustic. I was urban-oriented. I always felt more at home in trousers than in a dhoti." And it was a dhoti that Dev Anand had to wear in the film which also required him to sport a mustache. *Film India* certified this with, "From the players no one comes from within a mile of Dilip Kumar."

But Dev Anand vouches for Dilip's sincerity and hard work during the film. Says Dev, "Whenever I would go to meet the director Dilip would already be there before me discussing his scenes. He had a tremendous fervour to get things done the way he wanted them and it has stood him in good stead." Apart from zipping to and from Madras, Dev did not enjoy the experience, "I would land up on the sets, do my job and that's all! There was no rapport with the director or the unit. A chimpanzee was also there in the film and he ended up stealing the scenes."

In fact, not only did the "chimpanzee" end up stealing the scenes, it also ended up being the star of the show. Vasan shelled out a cool 15, 000 dollars for its services in the film in which it plays Agha's pet. Named Zippy the chimpanzee was trained and owned by Ralph Quinlan who had insured the animal for Rs 12.5 lakhs with Lloyds of

London. Zippy had been the star of several of television shows and films in America before being hired by Vasan in India. Which human star could stand such competition?

Dev Anand never made a film in the South again but Dilip must have established some rapport with "the director and the unit" for he did another film for Vasan, this time to help the producer who had run into huge losses following the failure of his last two films. *Paigham* (1959) is an underrated film, primarily because its progressive theme (of Labour versus Capital) is lost in the extensive "family drama" that was steadily becoming the forte of the Madras film in the 1950s.

Dilip Kumar as a swashbuckling hero in *Azaad*

Dilip Kumar played the factory worker who unwittingly becomes the leader of the factory workers much against the wishes of his loyal elder brother and thus gets alienated from his entire family. Painstaking as ever Dilip researched how the character of the labour leader would behave. "During that time I attended a meeting of labour leaders at Cawasji Jehangir Hall. George Fernandes was presiding and the way he delivered his speech was quite impressive. I came away with one point: a firebrand leader will always attack even if he doesn't have a case."

This time Dilip Kumar was pitted against another major star, Raaj Kumar, who was being lionised by fans for his stylish screen mannerisms. Once again Dilip Kumar's understated naturalistic acting blended well with the theme though Raaj Kumar's playing to the gallery may have got him some instant applause from the audience. Motilal, another naturalistic actor, cast as the mill owner who is eventually "humanised" by the events was an appropriate foil to the two other actors. Three performances are enough to place this film among the unforgettables.

The Madras family melodrama...Raaj Kumar and Dilip Kumar in *Insaniyat*

This was the time Dilip Kumar was more often in Madras than his home town of Bombay. One day he found himself in a queue to greet the then Prime Minister Pandit Jawaharlal Nehru who knew him quite well. When Panditji saw him in the queue he quipped, "What are you doing out here? Have you switched to Tamil films?" Dilip Kumar looked abashed and gave a tame answer, "Sir! Quite a few Hindi films are made in Madras, too!"

While *Devdas* was being edited Dilip Kumar would often visit the editing studio and strike up a conversation with the quiet bespectacled editor (and also Bimalda's chief assistant) Hrishikesh Mukherjee. Watching the editor at work in his quiet efficient way Dilip Kumar once suggested, "Why don't you direct a film?" The man did not even look up from his work but quietly said, "I want to but who will finance me?" The upshot was that the man wanted to make a film which was very much different from the kind of films being made then.

"What is the story?" Dilip wanted to know. Hrishikesh Mukherjee asked him to come home if he really wanted to hear the story. Curious, Dilip went over to where Hrishikesh Mukherjee was staying as a paying guest. Once the formalities were over Hrishikesh showed him the walls of the room he was staying in. They were scribbled with names and dates and, sometimes, small graffiti. "This," said Hrishikesh, "is the story I want to make. A film about a room which has been home to three couples ... each with their own story to tell."

Dilip Kumar was fascinated. "I'll do this film and never mind the money," promised Dilip. With Dilip Kumar willing to star in it, Hrishikesh Mukherjee managed to raise the money to start *Musafir*. Written by Ritwik Ghatak, *Musafir* told the story of the house in three segments: marriage, birth and death. Obviously Dilip Kumar starred in the third segment along with Usha Kiran and Daisy Irani. Dilip Kumar plays the lover who meets his estranged beloved and his child on his deathbed.

Far-fetched as it may sound many critics believe that *Musafir* takes off from where *Devdas* left off. In the Saratchandra novel, Devdas comes to Paro's doorstep but she is unable to take care of him – he dies before she even becomes aware of his presence. In *Musafir*, Devdas is resurrected as Raja and Uma prevails on him to stay with her so that she can care for him. Ironically *Musafir* uses the same Devdas team of cinematographer Kamal Bose, art designer Sudhendu Roy, writer Ritwik Ghatak and dialogue writer Rajinder Singh Bedi.

Usha Kiran and Daisy Irani with Dilip Kumar in *Musafir*

A special highlight of *Musafir* was a song sung by Dilip Kumar with Lata Mangeshkar ("**Laagi nahi chhute Rama chahe jiya jaaye**") under the baton of Salil Chowdhury – the first and last time Dilip Kumar sang for a film. Years later when he was asked if Lata Mangeshkar was nervous singing along with a star like Dilip Kumar he retorted, "On the contrary it was I who was nervous." Talking about his effort he says, "This song was sung and recorded with great abandon one evening or perhaps, one night. For me, at that time, it was quite an achievement. The words of that song are so nice, it's an old number and a very attractive one. In music, the beat worries me – if there are no beats, then I sing quite well; but if there is a beat, then I have to practice, do riyaz. And that takes time – nothing comes easy."

The Dilip Kumar-Naushad-S.U.Sunny combination which had given two major hits in the earlier part of Dilip Kumar's career (*Mela* and *Babul*) also came up with two major hits, five years apart: *Uran Khatola* (1955) and *Kohinoor* (1960).

Uran Khatola is a musical fantasy about a pilot (of an **uran khatola**) who crash-lands into a fantasy land and is befriended by a local girl. The queen of the land also falls in love with him and grows jealous when

Playing the violin for Daisy Irani in *Musafir*

she realises he is in love with one of her common subjects. Dilip Kumar and Nimmi (often referred to in the film industry as the female Dilip Kumar because of the number of times she has died in films) played the lovers who cannot meet on Earth while T.R.Suryakumari (fresh from the success of being crowned Miss Madras) played the beautiful but arrogant queen. This time it is Nimmi who dies leaving Dilip to mourn her till the climax when he dies, only to meet her in Heaven.

This trite and oft-told story of Love gained and lost is dressed up in grandeur and cloaked as a fantasy. Added to it was Naushad's foot

Meena Kumari and Dilip Kumar in *Kohinoor*

tapping music making it a popular hit. So popular, in fact, that the film was dubbed in Tamil as *Vanaratham* and released in the South to equally large audiences.

The final film of the decade was another fun-filled adventure in the best traditions of *Azaad*. It also starred the *Azaad* pair: Dilip Kumar and Meena Kumari. Maybe it was an attempt by the Dilip Kumar-Naushad-S.U.Sunny team to cash in on the success of *Azaad* – and a successful one at that! Crammed with songs, dances and gimmicks the film proved once and for all that the lead pair, known for their serious roles, could handle comedy with equal aplomb. Actually, quite ironical because with the pairing of the Tragedy King with the Tragedy Queen one would have expected at least one great tragedy but what the audience of the 1950s got were two really great song-and-dance extravaganzas.

When Dilip heard from Naushad that he would have to play the sitar for a song sequence in the film he was upset. "And how do you expect me to get the finger movements right for the close ups?" he queried. Naushad told him not to worry because Sunny would film the close ups on the hand movements of Ustaad Abdul Halim Jafar Khan, who had actually played for the song. Dilip did not say anything but he was not happy with the idea. He approached Ustaad Abdul Halim Jafar Khan and began to learn the sitar from him. When the film went on the floors and the scene was picturised a year later, Dilip was ready to play the sitar for the scene.

Another highlight of the film is the comic mirror gag between Dilip Kumar and the film's villain Jeevan, adapted with great success from the Marx Brothers comedy *Duck Soup* (1933) but first used in the cinema in the silent film *The Floorwalker* (1916). The hero takes refuge behind a mirror which unfortunately slips down. In order to escape notice he imitates every gesture that Jeevan makes so as to convince him that he is actually watching his mirror image. This gag has been copied in many films but no one with possible exception of Amitabh Bachchan (in the film *Mard*) has been able to carry it off with the same gusto as Dilip Kumar.

Chapter Eleven

– A Famous Court Case –

If the films of the first half of the 1950s were made against the background of the Dilip Kumar-Madhubala romance the films of the second half decade were made against the background of the Dilip Kumar-Vyjayanthimala romance. Beginning in 1955 they did a phenomenal seven films: *Devdas, Naya Daur, Madhumati, Paigham* (in the 1950s) and *Gunga Jumna, Leader, Sunghursh* (in the 1960s). It was obvious that they vibed well and had a special relationship. Dilip Kumar had worked with Vyjayanthimala in *Devdas* but she was a little wary of her big name co-star who had been billed by the press as moody and temperamental. Of course, Dilip charmed her off her feet on the sets of the film but it is doubtful if anything happened beyond it. The Dilip Kumar-Madhubala romance was still very much on but it was to come to a tragic end very soon.

But the *Naya Daur* story begins much before that. It was a story which no one wanted. It had done the industry rounds and had been rejected by all the top filmmakers of the day for being a "documentary" film ... till Akhtar Mirza narrated it to B.R.Chopra, who fell in love with it. Maybe it was the journalist in Chopra who reacted to the story's core message: progress is welcome as long as it is not at the cost of human aspiration. There had been socially relevant films in the past but no filmmaker had tackled a realistic subject of this complexity.

Even as he was hearing the story Chopra had set his heart on signing Dilip Kumar and Madhubala in the main leads but Dilip Kumar refused outright, saying that he had heard the story from Mehboob Khan and didn't like it one bit. Chopra decided to go ahead with the scripting and then narrate it once again to Dilip Kumar. The second narration – this time complete with script and dialogues in hand – took

Lovers reincarnated...with Vyjayanthimala in *Madhumati*

up four full hours but by the end of it, Dilip was also bowled over and
he signed on the dotted line.

Dilip Kumar's relations with Madhubala had soured but they were still close enough for them to be salvaged. Madhubala was also signed for *Naya Daur* and the film went on the sets. They must have shot for a bare ten days when Chopra brought up the matter of location shooting. The story was set against the background of a village in Bhopal. Even before launching the film Chopra had decided to shoot a majority of the film on the actual location. His unit had examined a few locales which were closer to Bombay but no one was satisfied. Chopra had therefore decided to shoot at a small village called Budhni, 250 kilometres from Bhopal.

When the matter of the location shooting was raised Attaullah Khan, who looked after all of Madhubala's matters, said a categorical "no". Now everyone in the film industry knew that Madhubala, because of her health and also probably because her father did not want to let go off his control over her, did not shoot on locations – the only time he had made an exception was for Shakti Samanta's *Insaan Jaag Utha*. Why Chopra had thought she would make an exception for him is not known but now faced with a major crisis he did not know what to do. Attaullah Khan insisted that the film could very well be shot in Bombay.

That was the time Dilip Kumar was also shooting for Bimal Roy's *Madhumati* and was on good terms with its leading lady Vyjayanthimala. Chopra did the only thing he could: he sacked Madhubala and signed up Vyjayanthimala. Had he done only that maybe the crisis would have remained a storm in a teacup but, smarting under rejection and losing the signing amount of Rs 30,000, he went a step ahead and gave full-page advertisements in the trade papers of the day announcing his film with the names of the lead pair. Madhubala's name was crossed out and Vyjayanthimala's name inserted. Not to be outdone Madhubala gave an advertisement in the same trade papers giving a list of her current starrers but with the title *Naya Daur* crossed out.

Matters would still have remained within the confines of the industry had not an enraged Attaullah Khan filed a case against B.R.Chopra for sacking Madhubala on flimsy grounds. The film could very well be shot in Bombay, he claimed. Chopra retaliated with a criminal case against Madhubala asking that she return his signing amount. The case came up for immediate hearing and the police constables outside the Girgaum Maigstrate's Court had a tough time handling the crowds who all wanted to see their favourite film stars battling it out.

In the courtroom presided over by Magistrate R.S.Parekh, the unsavoury details of the Dilip Kumar-Madhubala romance were laid bare before the viewing public who savoured the little details. Here was delicious gossip with a stamp of legal authenticity and from the mouths of the parties concerned. Matters reached a head when Dilip Kumar declared in open court, "I love this woman and shall love her till my dying day." The newspapers had a field day reporting all this. Eventually, everything ended tamely because Chopra did the gentlemanly thing of withdrawing the case.

The 300-strong unit went to Budhni and shot the film without any major mishap ... perhaps, a near mishap during the course of a race between a horse cart driven by Dilip Kumar and a bus, which forms the climax of the film. Recalls Chopra, "The horse cart was being driven at breakneck speed with Dilip Kumar holding the reins. At a crucial moment the reins slipped out of his fingers and we thought that was the end!! We abandoned the camera all set to go to Dilip Kumar's help but he had managed to keep his cool all through. He kept his footing, leaned out and managed to get back the reins. We all breathed a sigh of relief. The scene was retained in the film."

Yash Chopra, who was his brother's second assistant at that time, narrates an incident which is illustrative of Dilip Kumar's work culture during that period. When Yash approached Dilip Kumar for his dates ("Can you believe it? He had no secretary to look after his dates," remembers Yash), he said, "I am only doing two films: one with Bimal

With Vyjayanthimala in *Madhumati*

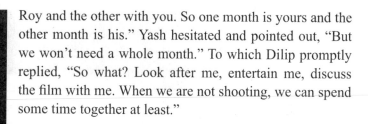

Roy and the other with you. So one month is yours and the other month is his." Yash hesitated and pointed out, "But we won't need a whole month." To which Dilip promptly replied, "So what? Look after me, entertain me, discuss the film with me. When we are not shooting, we can spend some time together at least."

And true to his word, Dilip Kumar once spent a whole day at his shack in Juhu performing the entire film for the Chopra brothers so that they could fine-tune his performance. It was this attention to detail, this obsession with not only his role but with the rest of the film which made Dilip Kumar the great actor that he is. Contrary to general understanding Dilip Kumar never cut down the roles of his co-stars to highlight his own; instead he saw that their role was equally powerful so that the resulting confrontation was a dynamic one. Like Ashok Kumar, he was not a born actor but worked exceedingly hard to cultivate his craft – watching, observing, learning and experimenting all the time. And this dedication is not to his work alone. He is equally committed to being a good human being first.

Yash Chopra remembers their days together on the location for *Naya Daur*, "Once we reached our second location in Poona we decided that we would take a good look at the location before actually shooting. We left in a jeep but Dilip preferred to stay back at the bungalow which had not been used in months. By the time we returned, the house had been spruced up. He had gone out and bought the pillows, bed-sheets and bed-covers. The badminton court had been cleared and the racquets had been purchased. All at his own cost! These are little things which tell you so much about the man."

Everything after that was almost an anti-climax and so

predictable. The film was released and was a superhit. B.R.Chopra had once again proved that his instinctive story sense was better than that of the other filmmakers in the film industry. He, quite literally, had his finger on the pulse of the times. The film had a message which was just right for the Nehruvian dream of making India a technological utopia. The film also appeals because it has an intrinsically human story: of a man who is fighting for a cause which has been given up as lost by the others.

One song from *Naya Daur* which became very popular was **"ude jab jab zulfay teri kawariyon ka dil dhadke"**. Normally the Urdu word **"zulfay"** refers to the feminine "bangs of hair" but in this song, lyricist Sahir Ludhianvi used the word with reference to Dilip Kumar's mop of hair which had been attracting attention right from his debut days. The reviewers made fun of Dilip's unruly hair-style but his fans adored it— the **"zulfay"** falling over his forehead and blowing freely in the wind became a fashion statement of the 1950s. In 1954, when Dilip Kumar led a procession of filmstars to collect relief for the victims of a flood, he discovered that by the end of the day, apart from the money he had collected, he was richer by a hundred combs. One interviewer who had been given a demonstration by Dilip Kumar on how his "zulfay" fell into place as if by magic, however differently his hair was combed, had this to say, "The much-maligned Dilip Kumar hair-style is more a creation of necessity than any new-fangled vogue of fashion."

By the early 1950s Dilip Kumar was a fashion role model on both sides of the border. Noted Pakistani journalist Khalid Hasan, best known internationally as the translator of the Saadat Hasan Monto stories into English recounts this tale. The famous Lahore-based portrait photographer M.Bhatti who ran his studio from the corner of the Mall and Beadon Road, was fond of telling a certain Dilip Kumar story. One day, a distracted young man walked into his studio and asked if he was M. Bhatti the photographer. He was, Bhatti told him. The young man, after some hesitation, pulled out a crumpled picture from his pocket, snipped out of a newspaper, and handed it to Bhatti

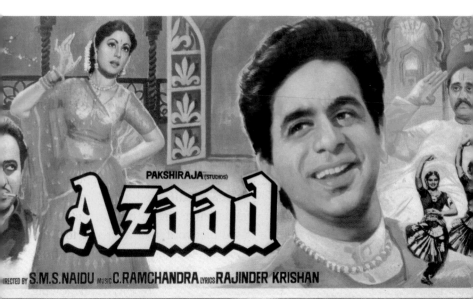

PAKSHIRAJA (STUDIOS)

Azaad

DIRECTED BY S.M.S.NAIDU MUSIC C.RAMCHANDRA LYRICS RAJINDER KRISHAN

BRO FILMS

Naya Dauz

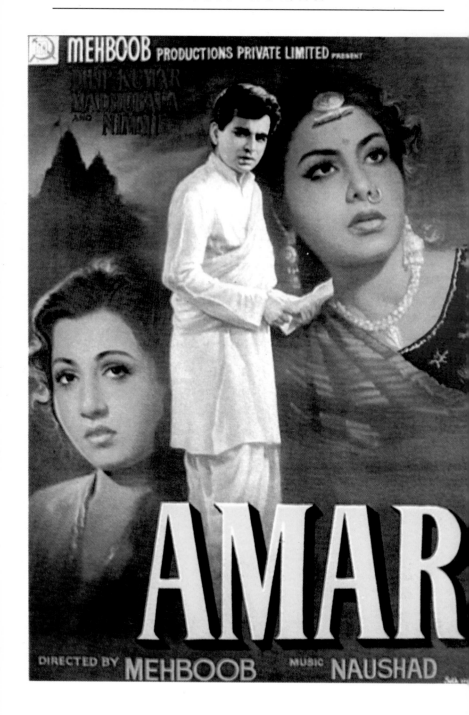

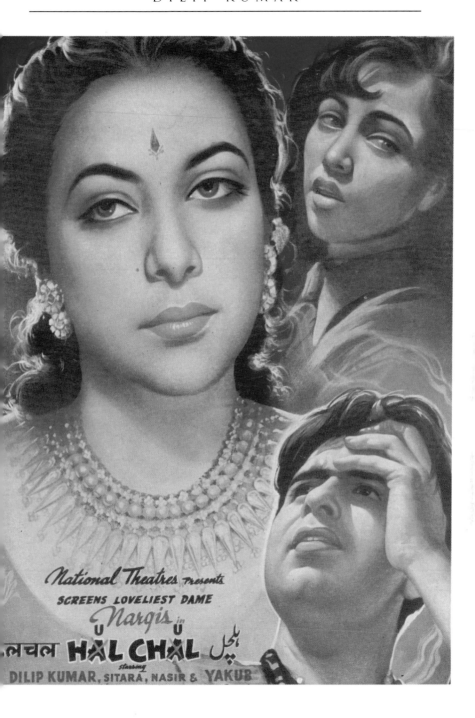

Dilip Kumar's public persona: Clockwise – with veteran journalist B K Karanjia; speaking at a function hosted by the National Association for the Blind; with Tabassum and Kalyanji; with Cabinet Ministers Sushma Swaraj and Yashwant Sinha

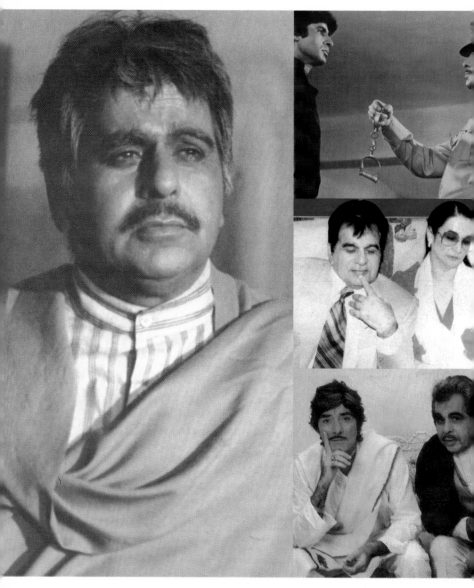

Dilip Kumar's character roles: Clockwise – with Amitabh Bachchan in *Shakti*; with wife Saira Banu; with Raaj Kumar on the sets of *Saudagar*: in a scene from *Mazdoor*

who had been looking at him all this time with increasing amusement. Bhatti flattened the picture with his hand on the table behind which he sat, looked at it carefully and asked, "So?" "Bhatti sahib, **meri bus bilkul aisi hi aik tasveer bana dena**," the young man said. Gently, Bhatti patted him on the cheek and answered, "**Barkhoodar, jis din tum meray paas Dilip Kumar wali shakal lay ke aaogay, uss din uss jaisi tasveer bhi banna doonga.**"

Even the stars who worked with Dilip jokingly questioned this great fan following – mostly female! Motilal who was Dilip Kumar's co-star in *Devdas* (playing the role of Chunilal) once asked the rhetorical question on the sets of *Devdas*, "What does Dilip Kumar have that I don't?" When no one answered, he ran his hand over his bald pate and said ruefully, "Maybe he has a little more hair. That's all!" To which everyone, including Dilip Kumar and Motilal, laughed.

The other film being shot at around this time was Bimal Roy's *Madhumati*, also starring Vyjayanthimala, with whom Dilip Kumar had begun to share special vibes. *Madhumati* was a story of reincarnation written to the song-and-dance formula then becoming popular in the film industry and was designed to appeal to the masses. The noted Marxist filmmaker Ritwik Ghatak had written the film for some quick money and was the total antithesis of the kind of films Ghatak had made in his native Bengal. He thought the whole film was a big joke and even went around saying, "I have written such a ghost story that Bimal Roy Productions will vanish forever."

Bimal Roy was in financial trouble since *Devdas* had not done too well on its first run. To top it, a large part of *Madhumati* was shot in Nainital over a period of 45 days so as to capture the authentic atmosphere of a hill station so necessary to heighten the mystery of the story. Thanks to the long schedule the film went over-budget by around Rs 8 to 10 lakhs. Dilip Kumar realised that Bimal Roy was tense and decided to do something about it. He asked Bimal Roy to call all his distributors for a preview followed by lunch. After lunch he told the distributors that the film had gone over-budget and that he would forgo Rs 70,000 of his remuneration to make up for it. One by one all the distributors came forward to contribute to the kitty and the deficit was made up.

As an improbable Roman in *Yahudi*

Madhumati was released and became an instant hit wiping out Bimal Roy Productions's accumulated losses as well as the complacent smile on the face of the Marxist filmmaker Ritwik Ghatak who could hardly have imagined the result of his labours. But by then Ghatak was already in Bengal shooting *Ajantrik* which was to reaffirm his status as a master of cinema and make him famous on the film festival circuit. Salil Chowdhury's lilting music combined effectively to create the eerie atmosphere required for the story – a combination which was copied to great effect in many of the suspenseful Manoj Kumar starrers of the 1960s like *Woh Kaun Thi* and *Anita*. In keeping with his new resolve to work in "lighter" films, Dilip Kumar does not die in the end and also gets to keep his lady-love – though in another lifetime!

With Nigar Sultana in *Yahudi*

Another Dilip Kumar starrer directed by Bimal Roy but for an outside production was released in the same year. After Bombay Talkies had closed down its last owner Savak Vacha had fallen on bad days. Dilip Kumar had agreed to help him out and had taken him to Bimal Roy. He wanted to make a spectacular production so as to recoup his losses. Bimal Roy had suggested the story of an amateur theatrical in which he had played the main lead: *Mishr Kumari* (*The Daughter of Egypt*), written by the noted playwright Agha Hashr Kashmiri. The film was quickly titled *Yahudi* and Meena Kumari and Dilip Kumar signed to play the lead role.

Yahudi was once again a costume drama against a very unusual background: Rome in the immediate post-Caesar days when a tyrannical Brutus was ruling the roost. The film's background required Dilip Kumar to wear the Roman toga (he plays a Roman wooing the Jewish girl) and a blonde wig. In spite of his outlandish appearance he gives a fairly credible performance. The final song of the film, when he has blinded himself as the punishment for having deceived the Jewish girl, is a connoisseur's delight: "**Yeh mera diwanapan hai ya mohabbat ka guroor.**"

Chapter Twelve

– The Third Milestone –

Dilip Kumar almost missed being in *Mughal-e-Azam* (1960). The film was first planned by K.Asif in the mid 1940s and its main financial backer was Shiraz Ali Hakim, who had actually given the young filmmaker a break with *Phool* in 1945. He also recommended Dilip Kumar for the role of Prince Salim but K.Asif, even then the master of spectacle, was not keen on signing up a rank newcomer. He knew that without stars no one would even look at the film. He, therefore, signed up Sapru, Nargis and Chandramohan to play the roles of Prince Salim, Anarkali and King Akbar. Asif also signed up the famous Urdu writer Imtiaz Ali Taj to script the film from his own original drama *Anarkali* written in the 1920s. Upcoming film writer Kamal Amrohi was signed to write the dialogues – the success of *Mahal* was still four years away. Anil Biswas, then at his height of creativity, was signed to score the music.

The film went on the floors, a few reels were even shot and then, the Partition of the country intervened. Shiraz Ali Hakim, who had led a public meeting in the early 1940s to felicitate Mohammad Ali Jinnah, thought he would be victimised for it and so, decided to migrate to Pakistan after selling the Famous Cine Studios and other assets to Jagmohan Rungta. Among other things and films, *Mughal-e-Azam* also came to a standstill.

When the project was revived in the early 1950s – thanks to the financial backing provided by the construction magnate and multi-millionaire Shapurji Pallonji – the scenario had changed completely. The actor selected to play King Akbar, Chandramohan, had died in 1949 at the young age of 44 years. Sapru was no longer the major star that he had been in the pre-Partition days. But another young actor who was making major strides in post-Independent cinema had just come within the K.Asif ambit. Dilip Kumar was playing the lead in his own production *Hulchul*, being directed by S.K.Ojha. But if Asif gained a hero on the sets of *Hulchul* he also lost his heroine there. Nargis and Dilip Kumar fell out while shooting for *Hulchul* and Nargis swore that it was the last film she would do with him. She backed out of *Mughal-e-Azam* and the hunt for a heroine was on again!

In the meantime the other stars were replaced. Prithviraj with his rich baritone voice was signed to play King Akbar. Ajit, whose own career as a leading man was coming to a close, was selected to play Durjan Singh while Asif's third wife Nigar Sultana was to play Bahar. Durga Khote was the only one who continued to play the role she had

A royal romance...with Madhubala in *Mughal-e-Azam*

been initially signed for: Jodhabai, Akbar's Rajput wife and Prince Salim's mother. The film went on the floor in real earnest in 1951 with no heroine in sight. The hunt was still on but something happened before another heroine could be found ...

Two other films on the same subject were announced. One was to be made under the M & T Studios banner and directed by Kamal Amrohi, who, thinking *Mughal-e-Azam* had been shelved, had sold the story to the studio. The other was to be produced by S.Mukerji under the Filmistan banner and directed by the veteran director Nandlal Jaswantlal. Asif had a measure of control over Kamal Amrohi and so his version was quickly brought to a halt. Not so the Filmistan version! The studio went ahead with Bina Rai and Pradeep Kumar playing Anarkali and Salim. The film, *Anarkali*, was released within a year and proved to be a major musical hit.

Things weren't any easier for Asif who had a much grander opera-style film in mind. A year of shooting later he finally found the heroine in one of Dilip Kumar's co-stars: Madhubala. She was Dilip Kumar's leading lady in two of his under-production films: Ram Daryani's *Tarana* (1951) and R. C. Talwar's *Sangdil* (1952). More than that, she was also the girl Dilip Kumar was in love with. She was the one about whom Dilip Kumar was to say in open court, "She is the only woman I have loved in my life and I shall love her till my dying day." The unfortunate fact which History hadn't disclosed as yet was that their love would run its course during the production of the film which would take a full nine years to make.

Khatija Akbar in her book on Madhubala writes, "During the making of *Mughal-e-Azam*, Dilip Kumar was in the habit of dropping by to see Madhubala even when he was not required for the day's shooting. He came on her sets and, if she was working, nothing was said. He stood watching; wordless glances were exchanged and he left, but his very presence was enough to transport Madhubala to a world of happiness. She looked forward to these few moments with

Scaling the heights of screen passion...Dilip Kumar and Madhubala in *Mughal-e-Azam*

all her heart, her eyes searching for him. When she saw him, her day was made."

This passion for each other translated very well onto the big screen – not only in the films they had done together but more so in an innately romantic film like *Mughal-e-Azam*. Many film observers of the day believe that the film captures the actual stages of Dilip's own romance with Madhubala. Which is why the romantic scenes of the film are some of the most intimate and erotic ever shot in Indian cinema – particularly the scene in which Dilip Kumar caresses Madhubala's ecstatic face with an ostrich feather. The story goes that Asif realized it wouldn't happen with Madhubala's father Attaullah Khan on the set. Asif took his PR man, Taraknath Gandhi, aside, and laid it down for him: "**Buddhe ko phutao. Jab tak buddha yahan rahega Madhu shooting nahin kar sakti**. Take this money, and play cards with him. Lose." It is said that Taraknath Gandhi spent the entire day in a remote office of the studio losing rummy hands to Khan while Asif filmed the erotic love scene.

But even as the scene was being shot it was apparent that the lovers had fallen out with each other. Why Dilip Kumar and Madhubala fell out with each other is a mystery. Unlike his other loves this affair could not have been socially forbidden. Both of them were Pathans. Both were compatible in age. Both were at the height of their film careers. More important, both were single and hence, there were no social impediments to their union. Many are of the opinion that it was Madhubala's fanatically stern father Khan Attaullah Khan who stood in the way of the marriage for fear of losing Madhubala, who was, after all, the breadwinner for the entire brood of sisters the old man had sired.

So, while the filming continued K. Asif grew more and more

A father weeps for his son...with Prithviraj Kapoor as Akbar in *Mughal-e-Azam*

impatient. The lovers were no longer talking to each other. If that wasn't bad enough, Madhubala's health began to deteriorate. She'd been diagnosed with "an enlarged heart with a hole in it." Paranoid to the core Attaullah Khan now even refused to allow his daughter to take part in important outdoor shots, out of fear she would get infected. Her illness was now so bad that she was suffering uncontrollable coughing fits. And yet, she continued to shoot.

Asif was a dreamer of huge ornate dreams but he was also a stickler for reality. When he wanted to show Anarkali in chains at the end of *Mughal-e-Azam* he got her to don real chains made of iron and which weighed kilos rather than the rubber chains which filmmakers generally use. And to think that Madhubala was in the final stages of the heart ailment which would eventually claim her life. By the time the climatic scenes were shot the romance was also at an end. So, not only were the chains real but the pangs of separating from one's beloved were also real because Dilip Kumar barely looked at

Madhubala and Dilip Kumar in *Mughal-e-Azam*

Mohabbat ki jhoothi kahani pe roye...Madhubala and Dilip Kumar in *Mughal-e-Azam*

Madhubala once the shots were done. And how true were the words of the song: "**Mohabbat ki jhoothi kahani pe roye**"

Madhubala suffered during these scenes but she refused to quit. For Madhubala the film was a challenge. Having come up the hard way in life she knew that whatever she had done as an actress till then would pale in comparison to the film which she was making. In the final run she wanted to be the best of the Anarkalis in Hindi cinema – better than Sulochana (Ruby Meyers) and Bina Rai. It was her passport to immortality. So, even after the romance had died down, she continued to give priority to the film – also hoping against hope that there would be some responsive spark from her former lover Dilip Kumar but he had moved on to other films ... and other women. In spite of this tragic end to a wonderful love story the film celebrated LOVE and the song "**Pyar kiya to darna kya?**" has, since then, become the anthem for defiant lovers in India.

Mughal-e-Azam was released on August 5, 1960 and instantly captivated the heart of audiences all over India. Historically the film was inaccurate. Prince Salim (later to become Jehangir) had accumulated a total of 18 wives during the course of his promiscuity but there never was an Anarkali in sight. But who cared! The film's ornate and opulent settings (in particular, the Sheesh Mahal set which is rumoured to have cost Rs 15 lakhs), its soulfully classical-based music (scored by Dilip favourite Naushad) and, above all, its larger-than-life performances have placed the film in the all-time Top Ten of Hindi cinema.

Asif claimed to have spent 20 years and Rs 1.25 crores in the making of *Mughal-e-Azam*. As usual *Film India*, giving a thumbs down to everyone in the film, had the last word. It wrote, "*Mughal-e-Azam* must be seen to realise how much a man can do in 20 years and with Rs 1.25 crores belonging to a Parsi multi-millionaire."

Chapter Thirteen

– *The Final Milestone* –

Gunga Jumna was the direct result of Dilip Kumar's not getting the Birju role in *Mother India*. The fact that Mehboob's film had proved to be a superhit pushed Dilip Kumar into proving his point: that the story could be told from the point of view of the bad son. Having decided the framework of his own role, the other aspects of the film fell into place without much trouble. By then Dilip Kumar was also itching to make a film on his own.

Those were the days when he was hard at work on Asif's magnum opus *Mughal-e-Azam*, which was being financed by Shapurji Pallonji, who had financed several industry stalwarts including V.Shantaram. Since Asif was taking his own sweet time to complete the project there was loose talk in the industry that he was taking his financer for a royal ride. Shapurji got panicky and was on the verge of pulling out when Dilip Kumar came to hear of what was about to happen. He rushed to Shapurji and offered not to take a single paisa as remuneration till the film was finished but entreated that Shapurji not pull out at this late stage. Shapurji was touched and agreed to stay on.

The incident brought Dilip Kumar closer to the builder-financer. One day he broached the idea of the film he had in his mind and Shapurji instantly agreed to finance it. *Gunga Jumna* was on! The story had already been written by Dilip Kumar. This was not the first time that Dilip Kumar had made a contribution in the writing of a film – this was only the first time he was taking official screen credit. The script was written by his former mentor and guide Nitin Bose, who was also to direct the film. Wajahat Mirza was roped in to write the dialogues which he did in chaste Hindi.

That was when Naushad suggested that a dacoit drama set in Uttar Pradesh would sound more authentic if the dialogues were in the local dialect. He suggested that they use the dialect of Eastern Uttar Pradesh, Purabi, but Dilip Kumar, at first, thought it would make him sound comic. Eventually Wajahat Mirza and Dilip worked on a few scenes and tried them out on some trusted and knowledgeable friends like Sashadhar Mukherji and Hiten Chowdhary. These two were particularly chosen because Hindi was not their mother tongue and they would be a good indicator of how a heterogenous audience would react.

The dialogues worked well and it was unanimously decided to make the film in Purabi. Dilip Kumar himself took Wajahat to the interiors of Uttar Pradesh so that they could pick up the nuances of the language. The process of transcribing the Hindi dialogue into Purabi was a painful one but even more painful was the process of saying

Nasir Khan, Dilip Kumar, Vyjayanthimala and Nazir Hussein
(back to camera) in *Gunga Jumna*

the dialogues. Ramamurthy Chaturvedi, an expert in folk languages, was especially hired to coach Dilip Kumar and Vyjayanthimala in the rendition of the language. The result was that even the South Indian Vyjayanthimala, who generally wrote down her dialogues in the Roman script, spoke the language with ease and conviction and won Filmfare's Best Actress Award for the year. Today it is impossible to think of any other actress in the role of Dhanno. Dilip Kumar publicly acknowledged Naushad's contribution to the dialogue at the Delhi premiere of the film, which set the fashion for Purabi/Bhojpuri-based dialogue in other later-day Hindi films – used more often in his films like *Ganga Ki Saugandh* and *Don* by the Allahabad-born actor Amitabh Bachchan.

Dilip's preparation for the film was very painstaking. Technicians with whom he had worked with have always vouched for Dilip's interest in the technical aspects of filmmaking. Dilip Kumar could well have directed the film but he brought in Nitin Bose from Calcutta. Having started his film career in the studio set-up of Bombay Talkies, Dilip was still enamoured with the idea of a hands-on producer like Himansu Rai who had full control over the content of his film. He looked upon the role of the producer as a fuller one than that of the director. Eventually, of course, he also ended up directing most of the film, using Nitin Bose as a kind of creative consultant to keep him on the right technical track.

To handle the ambitious production Dilip Kumar roped in Bimal Roy's Controller of Productions Premji who he had grown close to during the making of *Devdas* and *Madhumati*. Recalled Premji, "Dilip Kumar never forgets his friends and masters. Nitin Bose was brought back from Calcutta. M.I.Dharamsey was brought in as a sound recordist. V.Babasaheb with whim he had worked in *Daag* was signed as the cameraman though he had never worked in colour and the better-known Jal Mistry was available. In that film, there were at least 20 artistes who had fallen on bad days. Dilip Kumar made the film to pay his debts to those he had worked with in the past."

The film went into production with an outdoor shooting at Igatpuri. Dilip was then completing his work in *Madhumati* and also shooting for Asif's unending saga *Mughal-e-Azam*. Just then he received word from the veteran Madras-based producer S.S.Vasan. He wanted a favour: he wanted Dilip to give him continuous dates for his forthcoming film *Paigham*. He had incurred heavy losses on two of his previous films and was in great financial trouble. Dilip did not hesitate for a second and committed himself to the film. This further delayed *Gunga Jumna*.

Gunga Jumna was completed in early 1961 and, on submission to the Censor Board, promptly ran into rough weather. The censors had raised several objections to

With Vyjayanthimala in *Gunga Jumna*

the film, the principal one being that it could encourage dacoits and even provide tips to them on how a train dacoity was to be conducted. What went on to become the highlight of the film – both aesthetically and technically – was being objected to by the Censors. There were more than fifty such objections which, if accepted, would have ruined the character of the film.

Dilip answered the objections with a detailed note which the censors refused to read for the lack of time. The then Minister of Information and Broadcasting was Mr B.V.Keskar, a man who thought that films were corrupting influence on the nation. He had even banned the playing of film songs on All India Radio, thus compelling the national broadcaster to start Vividh Bharati in order to cater to popular demand. There was no reasoning with him. Finally Dilip Kumar decided to go to the highest authority in the land and argue his case. The then Prime Minister Pandit Jawaharlal Nehru gave him a patient hearing and finally the film was passed. After a year-long battle, *Gunga Jumna* was released at the fag end of the year in November 1961.

The film was a smash hit but there were several viewers who were unhappy that Dilip Kumar should spend his energies and talent on what they termed as "dacoit dramas". *Filmfare* gave voice to their discontent: "We congratulate Dilip Kumar for his rare art of motion picture production but not for the use to which he has put this art in his very first essay. This young man needs the right education in life's eternal values ..."

Probably the best summing up of the film came from contemporary Dev Anand who wrote in *Times of India* much later, "I am still mesmerized by *Gunga Jumna*. It's his best probably – an attacking aggressive performance which has become a text book on acting for generations of newcomers."

There were strong rumours that *Gunga Jumna* had been delayed so that another film based on the theme of dacoit reform – Raj Kapoor's *Jis Desh Mein Ganga Behti Hai* – could have a chance at the box office against Dilip Kumar's Technicolor drama which, according to popular opinion, was sure to sweep the box office. *Gunga Jumna* got three *Filmfare* awards that year but none of them were for Dilip Kumar – either as actor or producer. The awards for the Best Film and Best Actor went to *Jis Desh Mein Ganga Behti Hai* and Raj Kapoor.

A year later, Dilip Kumar won the Diploma of Honour for his memorable performance in *Gunga Jumna* at the 1962 Karlovy Vary International Film Festival. Two years later, in 1963, the film bagged the Silver Bowl for the Best Film at Boston, USA. Today, the film is as fresh as it was forty years ago when it was first released but Dilip Kumar never produced a film after *Gunga Jumna*.

Gunga Jumna

Chapter Fourteen

– *The Image Trap* –

Gunga Jumna (1961) was the second successive triumph for Dilip Kumar immediately after *Mughal-e-Azam* (1960). He was now 39 years old and had reached the height of achievement and creativity. Till then Dilip Kumar had had a dream run. A few films may not have done well but there were no serious threats to his position as an actor par excellence. On the contrary he had been flattered by the rise of quite a few imitators. He was fast becoming a role model for actors and he knew it. He knew he was well past his prime as the conventional leading man and so, even considered retirement from films.

Did he at that point consider a career in politics? *Film India* opening the review of his next film *Leader* snidely remarks, "Dilip Kumar has these days become an intellectual leader of film producers and sees dreams of becoming a political leader of the country at no distant date. Owing to his close association with V.K.Krishna Menon, the ex-Defence Minister of India, it is quite possible that Dilip Kumar might contest the next elections to fulfill his dream of being a political leader. His image of a leader as projected on the screen provides an important clue to the future designs of this man."

"His close association with V.K.Krishna Menon" refers to the 1957 election when Dilip Kumar along with Raj Kapoor and Dev Anand had canvassed for Krishna Menon who was then a young Left-wing intellectual and the "hope" of the youth in the country. At this late date one cannot be sure whether *Leader* was an advertisement of intention or just another addition to the Dilip Kumar oeuvre but it is a film which should never have been made because it became the first nail in the histrionic coffin of Dilip Kumar after a decade-long dream run. Even Dilip has confessed that after the successes of *Mughal-e-*

Azam and *Gunga Jumna* he became a little restless. He was not sure in what direction he was headed. Acting had become a little boring and repetitive considering the kind of roles he was playing in film after film. He had played around with the lighter kind of roles but they did not seem to give him enough histrionic sustenance.

Those around him advised him to move ahead into direction. The idea appealed to him but again he did not feel he was ready for it. "So I took the first tentative step. I began by writing my own story and dialogues for *Leader*. It was an interesting experiment though I admit I made quite a few mistakes. But it was fascinating. I learned a lot and more important, it gave me confidence," recalls Dilip. This is strictly not the truth because he had already been billed for the story of *Gunga Jumna* and everybody in the industry knew of his habit of "reworking" a film's dialogues. In fact, a senior actor like K.N.Singh had sarcastically remarked, "What's wrong? Is the dialogue writer dead?" when he saw Dilip Kumar going over the dialogues on the sets of *Shikast*.

Political ambitions... with Vyjayanthimala in *Leader*

Leader is the story of an idealistic journalist, played by Dilip Kumar, who disrupts political meetings and harangues politicians and their followers on what true patriotism is. One day a popular politician Acharya, played by Motilal, is shot and the journalist is arrested for his assassination. The journalist breaks out of jail to gather proof of his innocence.

On the face of it *Leader* was the ideal proposition to begin his non-histrionic career. It was being made by Sashadhar Mukherji who had a fantastic track record as a "hit" filmmaker and more important, he had always been a sympathiser of the actor right from his Filmistan days. This being the situation Dilip Kumar not only got to write the story but also have a say in its direction, which was officially credited to Mukherji's eldest son Ram. This was also the first time Dilip Kumar openly directed a film in public. Earlier he had only given "suggestions" to his director but now on certain occasions he actually directed several parts of the film. Many years later, Dilip Kumar confessed to an interviewer, "*Leader* was directed by S.Mukerji, Ram and yours truly."

Leader was not really a box office flop but it didn't do too well by Dilip Kumar standards – and also considering that a Dilip Kumar starrer was being released after a full three years. With three different directors directing the film, it lacked coherence and consistency but its main fault lay in the weak poorly crafted patchwork story, which was to become the norm of Hindi films in the 1960s. For the first time since he had started out in cinema Dilip Kumar did not have a strong story-base on which to base his character. It was probably this reason why he scurried back to familiar material in his next film, *Dil Diya Dard Liya*.

A.R.Kardar actually wanted to make a biographical film on Omar Khayyam and he even gave Dilip Kumar a signing amount of Rs two lakhs for it. However, after several rounds made to Dilip Kumar's Pali Hill house the star convinced him to drop the idea of making a film on Omar Khayyam and come up with something "more intimate like *Andaz*". Obviously the star wanted to play a "safe" role. Kardar had a leather-bound script based on the Emily Bronte novel *Wuthering Heights* but was not sure whether to hand it over because Dilip had already played the Heathcliff role twice before: *Aarzoo* and *Hulchul*.

Heathcliff is a character who seems to have fascinated Dilip Kumar for, apart from playing it straight in three films, he has used shades of the character in several other films (*Aadmi*). Heathcliff is a man on the edge: spiteful, mad, insecure and thirsting for revenge. Dilip Kumar added the dimension of the tormented lover who has been denied his rightful love and hence seeks a bloody revenge on the inhabitants of Wuthering Heights. This was to remove the essential negativism of the role and attract audience sympathy by giving the character a justification – so essential for the hero of a Hindi film. Dilip, however, says that he did not "insist on the remakes, they just happened".

In truth, however, Dilip has always preferred to play the hero with a touch of negativism: recall *Babul, Deedar, Shikast, Devdas* and, the most notable of them all, *Amar*. In each of his early films, Dilip's character toys with his female protagonists, leading them along, making them think that he cares for them when he actually does not, thus leading them to tragedy: Bela (Nargis) in *Babul*, Champa (Nimmi) in *Deedar*, Nimmi again in *Amar*, Chandramukhi (Vyjayanthimala) in *Devdas*. He was caught in an image trap but did not realise it till it was too late. Much later he confessed, "One gets caught, one is trapped, one doesn't get out till the audience doesn't like it anymore. There's repetition, there are gimmicks ... the persona becomes a cult by itself."

At that moment, however, the idea of playing a familiar character on familiar territory probably elated him but now he did not look upon himself as a mere actor. He wanted a stake in the making of the film but he was still not prepared to come fully out in the open. Recalled

Kardar, "After handing over the script to him, I did not see his face for six months. When he did get back he had changed 80 scenes. I could do nothing. I had to go ahead. I couldn't back out since commitments had been made to my financiers, distributors and other artistes."

Unfortunately Kardar's troubles did not end there. The shoot began in Mandu, once the capital of what was then Malwa and is today western Madhya Pradesh. On the sets, Dilip Kumar insisted on taking over the reins from the more experienced Kardar. He became a dictator on the sets, canning take after take and often rejecting the next day what he had shot on the previous day. Co-star Pran, however, has fond memories of the film. He feels that "Dilip Kumar helped me a lot with my performance. He never objected to retakes, even if the other artiste was calling for it to improve his performance." Thus he expended four lakh feet of film in four years and was finally all set to edit the film. Commented Kardar, "I could have made eight films from that footage. Dilip Kumar was my Waterloo."

His most mature performance...with Waheeda Rehman in *Aadmi*

Dil Diya Dard Liya flopped and Kardar was heartbroken and worse, ruined. His career had come to a dead-end. Kardar recalled, "I decided to work with Dilip Kumar only because my first choice Raj Kapoor was unavailable for a year and also because my wife Bahar was keen that I work with Dilip Kumar, who was a great favourite of her sister's husband Mehboob Khan. Dilip Kumar has never given happiness to anyone, he has always made life difficult for filmmakers."

Asked to comment on it years later, Dilip Kumar said, "That was unfortunate. At one time, he was considered Bombay's biggest movie tycoon but his decline had started – six to seven of his films had failed at the box-office. His craftsmanship did have class but he would often try to cut corners and finish a picture on a shoestring budget. He overlooked the advance of film technology and the market demands and was, therefore sadly left behind."

If *Dil Diya Dard Liya* ended Kardar's career, it also put temporary brakes on Dilip Kumar's career. Two releases in six years and both flops. Dilip Kumar fans began to think hard. Had their idol reached the end of his limits? Should he have retired at the height of his fame soon after *Mughal-e-Azam* and *Gunga Jumna*?

But Dilip Kumar had one more trick up his sleeve. He was, at that very moment, acting in the first double role of his life. But before that something else happened ....

Chapter Fifteen

– The Eligible Bachelor Succumbs –

The news originated in the grapevine, passed through the gossip magazines and was picked up by the mainstream newspapers. After all, it was no ordinary news item. The impossible had happened. The most eligible bachelor in filmdom – a little way past his prime, no doubt – was getting married to a nubile actress who had hit the headlines with her very first film.

Had it been Waheeda Rehman it would not have shocked too many people. She had played the lead opposite him in *Dil Diya Dard Diya* and was his co-star in two more films which were currently on the sets: *Ram Aur Shyam* and *Aadmi*. What's more, there were also some whispers about a budding Dilip Kumar-Waheeda Rehman romance though it could really mean nothing because tongues in the film industry tend to wag the moment a new pair is formed – it is an occupational hazard. Instead it was the nubile young actress with whom he had never acted before: Saira Banu, daughter of yesteryear actress Naseem Banu, who was barely a year older than Dilip Kumar, and who had missed being his co-star in *Footpath*. Interestingly, had the casting come about Dilip Kumar would have become the only actor to have acted opposite both a mother and a daughter.

Saira Banu was hardly Dilip Kumar's choice of the ideal bride. Writing in *Filmfare* in 1953 on 'What I Want From Life', Dilip Kumar had written: "If I marry I want a cheerful partner who will not draw me away from my duties towards my family, my friends and from humanity at large. I do not want an ultra-modern girl with frivolous notions about propriety in living, false ideas and shabby values about the things which matter in life, such as human integrity. I also wish that from time to time she should leave me to myself and not cross

examine me as if I were a convict."

But for Saira it was definitely a childhood dream come true. She confessed, "Yusuf Saab had always been a family friend but when I first saw him in my early teens (I was 13 or 14 years old then) I set my heart on him and I knew that this was the man for me. I knew I wanted to be Mrs Dilip Kumar."

Saira Banu is the daughter of Naseem Banu, a major star of the 1930s and 1940s, and her estranged husband Mohammad Ahsan, who, along with his actress-wife, had set up a production company Taj Mahal Pictures in the 1940s. Saira was born on August 23, 1941 at Mussoorie. After Partition Ahsan migrated to Pakistan while Naseem stayed on in India. Later Naseem settled down in London where Saira and her brother Sultan were educated. Returning from London in 1959 she made her debut in Hindi films opposite Shammi Kapoor in *Junglee*.

The film was a superhit and Saira was established as a superstar. Other hit films like *Bluff Master, April Fool, Door Ki Aawaaz, Aao Pyar Karen* and *Pyar Mohabbat* with some of the industry's top leading men followed. But her dream to work opposite Dilip Kumar remained unfulfilled because he kept refusing films with her on the pretext that she was too young to work with him. But she continued to work with the other popular leading men of the day. Her first film with Rajendra Kumar *Aayee Milan Ki Bela* was a great success and they followed it up with the signing of *Aman* and *Jhuk Gaya Aasmaan*. As is wont to happen the on-screen romance spilled over into real life and the gossip magazines began to write about them.

Naseem Banu, no stranger to the behind-the-screen world of films, began to fret about the association – particularly since Rajendra Kumar was not only a Hindu but also a married man with three children. Dilip Kumar and her long-time mentor Sashadhar Mukerji were roped in to "talk sense" to Saira. Reluctant at first, Dilip finally gave in to

Naseem's persistent requests – probably because Sashadhar Mukerji had also been roped in to do likewise – and he is said to have had several talk sessions with Saira Banu.

Matters reached a head at Saira's birthday party on August 23, 1966. Dilip Kumar had been invited but had already sent in a note of apology for his inability to attend. At the height of the party in walked Rajendra Kumar with wife in tow. This upset Saira who had kept herself in control over the last few weeks. Sensing that matters could get out of hand, Naseem Banu rushed over to Dilip Kumar's house and begged him come over and save the situation. Cornered and unable to say "no", Dilip agreed and went over to attend Saira's birthday. Saira was thrilled to see her childhood idol at her birthday and a public spectacle was avoided.

Six weeks later came the announcement that surprised the nation: Dilip Kumar and Saira Banu were to be engaged on October 2, 1966. What had transpired behind the scenes to have brought about this new state of affairs?

Apparently on the day of the party Dilip Kumar had been requested to once again speak to Saira about her foolish involvement with a married man. As Dilip Kumar gave argument after argument Saira is said to have brought his arguments to a standstill with one simple statement: "I will stop pursuing him if you agree to marry me!" What happened after that one will never really know but the upshot was that Dilip Kumar agreed to marry her.

Soon after the engagement the couple went to Calcutta – Dilip Kumar to attend the script sessions and location hunting of *Sunghursh* and Saira to shoot for *Jhuk Gaya Aasman*. The marriage had been fixed for November 4 but there was so much keen anticipation of the marriage that wherever the couple went they were literally **gheraoed** by crazy fans who wanted to see them together. The time came when they had to be literally smuggled in and out of the hotel they were staying in. Eventually it was decided to bring ahead the date of the marriage in the hope that the craze to see them would die down once they were married.

The marriage, as was to be expected, was one of the most glamorous in filmdom. Raj Kapoor had married Krishna much before he became a film star and Dev Anand had married Kalpana Kartik in a quiet, almost secret, marriage ceremony on the sets of *Taxi Driver*, the film they were shooting. Dilip Kumar's marriage was different. He was already a major star and the years of anticipation had added a keen-ness to fan curiosity. No less a person than Prithviraj Kapoor led

Married at last... with Saira Banu on the day of their wedding

the **baraat** and Dilip's contemporaries Raj Kapoor and Dev Anand led the mare on which the bridegroom was seated. Pran, the villain of the day and Dilip's co-star in nine films, had to travel on someone else's air ticket to make it to Bombay in time for the marriage. The entire film industry seemed to have gathered there and so were the fans who had lined the street from Dilip Kumar's house to Saira Banu's house, just a short distance away. The celebrations went on till early morning – so much so that the newly-married couple had to forgo the traditional **suhaag raat**.

Soon after the marriage the couple flew to Madras where Dilip Kumar was shooting for B. Nagi Reddy's *Ram Aur Shyam* in which he was playing the first double-role of his career. Obviously it was to be a working honeymoon but Saira, now that she had snapped up the most eligible bachelor in filmdom and the man of her childhood dreams, did not mind.

While at Madras Saira discovered that the man she had married, in spite of his serious demeanour, was actually full of pranks. As a concession to the privacy of a newly-married couple they had been given a huge dilapidated bungalow to live in.

They were both fond of after-dinner walks and they would take these in spite of the wilderness around the bungalow. Often, as Saira walked along the deserted road, Dilip would creep up from behind and in an eerie voice say, "Do you really think that you are walking with your husband?"

Or he would say, "Look there is that woman up there on the tree and she is calling out to me. Her hands are getting longer and longer."

Often, after the lights had been put out, he would stealthily leave the house and throw stones at the windows.

These things would really frighten Saira.

Saira Banu continued to work in films even after her marriage and Dilip Kumar did not ask her to quit. Some films were quietly dropped in deference to Saira's new status. One such film was K.Asif's Rajendra Kumar-Saira Banu starrer *Sasta Khoon Mehenga Pyaar*. K.Asif, who was married to Dilip Kumar's sister Akhtar, allowed the film to die a silent death because he did not want to embarrass Dilip – though the film had shaped up very well and was guaranteed to be a hit. Bits of this film can still be seen as part of a compilation film made by Shahab Ahmad, *Film Hi Film*. Saira continued to make films – and very successful ones like *Herapheri* and *Victoria No 203*. She also acted with Dilip Kumar in three films: *Gopi* (1970), *Sagina* (1974), *Bairaag* (1976). And then, suddenly at the height of her career she decided to quit films.

Talking to *Screen* years later she gave the reason. Once, soon after their marriage, when she was shooting for Ravi Chopra's debut film *Zameer* with Amitabh Bachchan, she was on her way to Kashmir via Delhi. Dilip had just flown into Delhi to catch up with some personal work. Since they had a couple of hours they met at the airport. Just when they had to part and catch their respective flights she realised that she wanted to stay back and spend some more time with Yusuf Saab. That was the instant she "felt that I was not giving enough time to the marriage and that was the day I decided that **ab kaam nahin karoongi**. Enough! I'll stay at home".

Of course she has often regretted the decision at leisure because, as she says, "I realised that the best thing a woman can do is to stick to her job as well as her marriage. Because I realised that the years when I was married and simultaneously working were maybe the best years of my life. It is best that the woman keeps working and has an identity of her own."

After marriage, Saira discovered that Yusuf Saab is a totally dependent man. She remembers, "He is like a poet, a dreamer. You have to fend for him all the time. He's not childish but child-like.

So utterly dependent! He does not know where his handkerchief is or where his cheque book is. He doesn't know where his cuff links are. With this man you have to do everything for him. And it is not because he does not know how to do anything, but just that he is a totally dependent man. I try to be his sustenance but I don't know how far I succeed."

Saira Banu and Dilip Kumar in *Sagina*

Saira recalls the first time she cooked for Yusuf Saab, "While I am fond of eating I am not a very good cook. Both my mother and grandmother were excellent cooks. I cooked for Yusuf Saab for the first time in Chennai. I made **aloo mutter** and garlic chicken under the supervision of my mother. Yusuf Saab was very delighted with my cooking primarily because I had made it with a lot of love."

In the matter of food, she says that "Yusuf Saab is basically a green vegetable person. He loves **gobi ke kofte** and **baingan ki burhani sabzi** and the **salan unke hisaab se hona chahiye**. It should not be too oily or too spicy. He also loves papayas and bananas. Occasionally he goes on a **biryani** binge and then we have an open house. On the other hand I am a non-vegetarian. My mother tried to inculcate the habit of eating green vegetables and fruits. I didn't quite like it but now I have got used to having even **turai**."

For Dilip Kumar his family has always been the centre of his existence. After the death of his parents early in his career he had always shown great respect for elder brother Noor Mohammad though he was not as close to him as he was to Ayub. Unfortunately Ayub, always in delicate health, passed away of kidney failure in 1954. His elder sister Apaji was the "mother" to the family and everything in the Khan household was conducted under her eagle but benign eye. All the younger siblings were given an excellent education though none of them ever made a mark away from Dilip Kumar. Ahsan and Aslam studied in the United States but while Aslam settled down with an American wife Ahsan returned to India and became a producer. Nasir Khan, of course, carved out a career for himself as a film star but after Partition he too slipped from the position. Dilip tried to help him regain his lost star value but it was not to be.

Thus, Dilip Kumar had always wanted to marry a girl who would adjust with his family and live with them amicably. Recalls Saira, "He has always had a big family with lots of brothers and sisters and some of whom have unfortunately been widowed or divorced and his house has become a kind of a family house. Everyone would be perpetually either coming or going. When he saw that I was terribly uncomfortable in the family home because of the onslaught of people all the time, to the extent that I fell ill he was good enough to pick me up from there and bring me here to my own place. That was a great thing he did and his biggest gift to me is that he will let me stay with my own people."

While this may seem as a major adjustment for Dilip Kumar, there has been some adjusting on Saira's part too. "When you are married to a Pathan everything goes his way. It is not so much a matter of compromise but of adjustment. And if you are a woman you have to give in," she says with a smile.

As is to be expected Dilip Kumar has had the last word on their marriage, "I used to lead a wild lifestyle with no one to control me. I'd be on an outdoor location for a month and I'd be upto all sorts of **awaragardi**. Marriage has been a stabilising factor. I didn't surrender my freedom at one go, I've forfeited it slowly but surely."

Chapter Sixteen

– The Ageing Hero –

Saira Banu proved to be Dilip Kumar's proverbial lucky charm. The career which had begun to show signs of floundering steadied and came up with four smash hits: *Ram Aur Shyam* (1967), *Aadmi* (1968), *Sunghursh* (1969) and *Gopi* (1970). Of these, at least the first three were solid performances to be proud of.

Ram Aur Shyam, a remake of the Tamil film *Enga Veetu Pillai*, was a reworking of *The Prince And The Pauper* tale with a twist of *A Comedy of Errors*: the focus here is on highlighting the merry mix-up created by the two identical personalities. Dilip Kumar had played lighter roles before but *Ram Aur Shyam* was in the purest traditions of slapstick. Playing the first double role of his life Dilip Kumar went to town with it. While Shyam was the boisterous buffoon, Ram was a delightful parody of Dilip Kumar's own earlier "whipped dog" roles. The film provided the impetus for other double-role explorations in films like *Ghazab* (Dharmendra), *Seeta Aur Geeta* (Hema Malini), *Angoor* (Sanjeev Kumar) and *Chaalbaaz* (Sridevi).

Vyjayanthimala and Mala Sinha were to have played the main roles and a signing amount of Rs one lakh had also been given to Vyjayanthimala but there was a mix-up in the dates and a schedule was lost. Producer Nagi Reddy finalised a fresh set of dates with Dilip Kumar and then, approached Vyjayanthimala for her dates. Angry that she was being asked to adjust her dates with those of Dilip Kumar she is supposed to have said, "If Dilip Kumar is Dilip Kumar then I am Vyjayanthimala." Finally Waheeda Rehman was brought in to play the role and Mumtaz got the chance of a lifetime to act opposite Dilip Kumar – and she did the role with great verve and vivacity.

Dilip Kumar as Shyam in *Ram Aur Shyam*

By now, of course, Dilip was openly doing the director's job. As Pran notes in his autobiography, "Dilip Saab used to do the actual work even though the name as director was someone else's. And he used to help all co-artistes with their work." The approval is not only implicit because Pran echoes what Dilip always believed, "Until all the artistes in the scene have given of their best, the scene cannot come off well."

Aadmi, based on the Tamil Sivaji Ganesan starrer *Alayamani*, was vintage Dilip Kumar with a controlled angst-ridden performance of a man whose intense jealousy ruins the life of his closest friend (Manoj Kumar) and sweetheart (Waheeda Rehman), not to speak of the repercussions it has in his own life. Dilip Kumar played the role of a man with two faces: the public philanthropic face hiding the intensely complex man whose petty-minded unsharing nature has already caused the death of a friend in his childhood. It is the performance of an actor in full bloom and it is matched by the performances of both Manoj Kumar and Waheeda Rehman.

During the making of the film many pundits predicted that the film was doomed to failure and that A.Bhim Singh was on the verge of apoplexy. Their predictions were based on the fact that the film starred Dilip Kumar and Manoj Kumar, both of whom were known to constantly interfere in the work of the director and the making of the film. Says Manoj Kumar, "*Aadmi* was the effort of one man alone, Dilip Kumar, and mind you it was not interference like most people say. It was the dedication and the devotion of the man to his job which he had taken up and he wanted to see it through to the best of his ability." What Bhim Singh had to say about it has not been recorded for posterity because the pundits were proved wrong and the film was not only very coherent but also a super hit.

Sunghursh was a Romeo-and-Juliet tale retold against the backdrop of two warring families of **thugs** (thieves who ritually murdered travellers as sacrifices to the Goddess Kali), thus placing the film firmly in the early 19th century. Dilip Kumar plays the young man who tries to end the family feud with tragic consequences. The feudal

Sunghursh

background gave the film a character which allowed Dilip Kumar to play his actual age. Starring opposite him was Vyjayanthimala but their ardour had so cooled down that the two stars were not even on talking terms. But being the professionals that they are it is not noticeable anywhere in the film – not even the romantic scenes. The highlight of the film is, of course, the confrontation scenes between an ageing Dilip Kumar and a young Sanjeev Kumar. Even before the film was released, stories of the young actor holding his own against the legendary Dilip Kumar were doing the rounds and much of the success of the film emanates from this sporting gamesmanship.

The film was scripted by director H.S.Rawail's wife Anjana Rawail from a novel by the noted Bengali litterateur Mahashweta Devi.

Interestingly, Philip Lutgendorf, Professor of Film at the University of Iowa, finds in the film a subtext which wouldn't strike most Indians, "However, its ultimate concern to reunite two sundered brothers (actually, as in the Mahabharata, first cousins, and played by a Muslim and a Hindu actor) suggests a subtext that isn't really about Hinduism at all, but about the communal divide that haunts post-Partition India, here projected into the past and disguised within an exclusively Hindu milieu."

Gopi, also directed by A.Bhim Singh, is nothing more than an extension of the *Shyam* character: a boisterous buffoon who would rather cavort around with the village belles and get up to all sorts of mischief rather than help out his elder brother (Om Prakash) and sister-in-law (Nirupa Roy) whom he actually worships. The hero is shown with an impossible heart of gold and it is only the villain-created misunderstanding which can take him away from his house. Gopi leaves the house but finds shelter in a zamindar family under the warm matronly wings of "maaji" (Durga Khote).

Dilip Kumar was sharing the screen with Om Prakash after almost 15 years. Om Prakash had played the bumbling police constable in *Azaad* and the comedy pairing of the two actors had caught the fancy of the audience. But something happened on the sets of *Azaad* and the two never acted together again. The story goes that Om Prakash happened to see *Aadmi* in Madras and was so captivated by Dilip's performance that he instantly rang up the thespian and congratulated him. The misunderstandings and the distance of almost a decade-and-a-half melted away. The result was the fantastic performance that the two great actors gave as brothers in *Gopi*. Om Prakash also played a significant role in *Sagina*. What the audience lost in the intervening years we shall never know.

Dilip Kumar was nearing fifty but the character required him to play a young man in his early twenties. No amount of excellent acting could cover up this mismatch which shows up very clearly in the film. This is the first film in which he shows the signs of his true age. The film is also an excellent example of what happens to a rudderless actor. While Shyam was an intrinsic part of *Ram Aur Shyam*, Gopi is a larger-than-life caricature and it is obvious that the rest of the film is being made to revolve around this one character. The film was a hit at the box office but as a film it fails to rise to Dilip Kumar's own stringent standards.

Dastaan is an unabashed remake of *Afsana*, which had been

With Leena Chandavarkar in *Bairaag*

offered to Dilip Kumar way back in the 1950s. Dilip Kumar then had thought that the role – a double role – was too much of a challenge for someone who was "starting out". He also sincerely felt that the role required a much more mature actor and so, he asked B.R.Chopra to sign a more experienced actor. The film was completed with Ashok Kumar playing the lead but producer-director B.R.Chopra swore that he would remake it again with Dilip Kumar. *Dastaan* was the result!

Dilip Kumar once again plays a double role: the sober studied judge and the frivolous fun-loving actor. It is an excellent contrast in types and Dilip Kumar's delineation of character is superb but he cannot go beyond the film's old-fashioned oft-repeated theme. Chopra, astute as ever, realised what had gone wrong much later, "When we made *Afsana* it was a novel theme, off-beat and bold. But 23 years had passed since and the novelty had worn off. We forgot this basic factor and I think it was this which was responsible for its failure. We went in for a remake at the wrong time."

Though the famed Bengali director Tapan Sinha claims that "I could not think of anyone else the moment I completed the script of *Sagina*", there is no denying that a younger Dilip Kumar would have done greater justice to this (then) timely story of a factory worker who is manipulated by the factory's owners into becoming a labour leader. The labour leader preens at his new status, thus alienating his colleagues who had once looked upon him as their own. Eventually he is tried in a people's court and found guilty.

Sagina (Hindi)/*Sagina Mahato* (Bengali) is a film which should have been made at least ten years before it was – primarily because the story, with its strong Naxalite overtones, had become anachronistic by the time the film was made. More than that, a sober elaboration of the central character would have worked much better but Dilip Kumar once again came up with a boisterous gallery performance when he should have gone back to search for clues in his past characters. One wonders what a vintage Dilip Kumar would have done with the film.

Bairaag was the last of Dilip Kumar's overtly romantic roles. He played a triple role in the film: a father and two sons, when he should have played only the father. This was the first time that a leading man has played a triple role in a film (barring Sanjeev Kumar's unusual nine roles in *Naya Din Nayi Raat,* which had also been offered to Dilip but who had content himself with speaking the opening commentary introducing the film). This is also the first film of another Dilip Kumar clone: Kadar Khan, whom Dilip Kumar called after seeing his plays. Dilip Kumar's younger brother Nasir Khan puts in a cameo as a doctor who treats the father – playing a role for the first time after *Gunga Jumna*. Ironically Nasir Khan passed away following a massive heart attack in 1976 soon after he had completed his work in *Bairaag*.

Another interesting sidelight of this film was that *The Economist* used a photograph from this film with Dilip Kumar and Saira Banu on the cover (2001) to illustrate its story on ten years of liberalisation in India. What a tribute to a flop film!!

The film was said to have been directed by the sensitive Asit Sen but in actual fact was put together by Dilip Kumar himself. By then the chorus of voices talking about Dilip Kumar's constant interference in the technical departments of the film had become louder and even his fans could not ignore them. Under the guise of perfectionism and professionalism what was happening was that Dilip Kumar was reshooting and remaking each one of his films.

Dilip Kumar's defence was a simple, "Look, the audience appreciates qualitative work even in poor films, the actor stands out more sharply so when the product is of superior standard. I've never interfered with a competent director. When I see things going awry, I've suggested alterations which would be more effective. I have been willing to take "no" for an answer. There has to be negotiation in a team. I wouldn't call this interference."

In spite of all this posturing there is no denying that the later films of this period (*Gopi, Sagina, Dastaan*) are all projects which failed to

Plotting a revolution...Dilip Kumar in *Sagina*

reach their full potential in spite of superb plots and tailor-made roles. Was Dilip Kumar responsible? Or were they just ill-fated projects? In any case Dilip Kumar had made his decision. He had had enough! He announced his retirement sending shock waves throughout the industry.

He said, "I had begun to sense a stagnation in my work. I was fed up with the same roles in the same monotonous films. The time had come to make a clean break rather than slide into mediocrity. So I gave up films completely even though I had no goals for the future. I didn't know what I was going to do ... How I was going to spend my time ... But then, all of life's a gamble, isn't it?"

Chapter Seventeen

– The Public Life of a Private Man –

Dilip Kumar was not going to make any more films as an actor but he was still an active man who could do a full day's work. What then was he going to do? The answer to that question came soon enough because there were people who were interested in using the brand equity of that name and all that it meant to the man on the street. Dilip Kumar had always been an advocate of the less fortunate. Says Dilip, "I have always believed that people as fortunate as us should do something for the less blessed as there is so much misery in the world. It is impossible to eradicate misery completely but if we can do even a little to lessen it the world becomes a lot more worthwhile place to live in."

He has never wanted to be a mere film star. Dilip Kumar was at the forefront of film industry causes right from the 1940s when the film industry formed the Film Functions Committee. He along with Raj Kapoor and other film personalities worked assiduously for the victims of the Bengal Famine. Within the film industry he, along with Dev Anand and Raj Kapoor, formed the Screen Actors Guild and spoke up for junior artistes all through his career. Recently in 1990 he chaired the Committee of Hope and helped stage a concert for junior artistes.

In 1962 when the Indo-China War broke out he formed the Film Industry Defence Committee. He not only organised star processions to collect funds but also organised shows in the bitter-cold snow-clad mountains of Siachen to entertain the **jawans** on the border. In 1965, after the Indo-Pak War he along with Raj Kapoor and Dev Anand raised funds for war widows.

More than that, he has always been on the forefront of public life right from the late 1950s. In the 1957 and 1962 Lok Sabha General Elections he canvassed for V.K.Krishna Menon of the Congress along

A public life: Top – with Chandrashekhar (standing), Ameen Sayani and
David planning a film function; bottom – At the swearing-in ceremony for
the Sheriff of Bombay

Clockwise – with Shiv Sena pramukh Balasaheb Thackeray; with Mother Teresa; with Raj Kapoor during an exhibition cricket match

with Raj Kapoor and Dev Anand. He did not canvass for him in the 1967 General Elections because Krishna Menon had distanced himself from the film industry and its problems during the intervening years. But that did not stop him from being a Congressman all his life.

Dilip Kumar has an intuitive understanding of the political process and the politics that make up India but he has always shied from active politics because he did not want to sully his hands. He felt that he would lose the adulation of his fans if he ever joined active politics, probably Amitabh's experience in the arena kept him away from politics and politicians since then. However, in 1981 he returned to public life when he was appointed Sheriff of Bombay. He used this public office to bring succour to countless common people of Bombay who would have otherwise languished in anonymity.

He would have continued with his public work but "even social work, after a while, did not hold my attention for long. I missed my acting." But while continuing to act he was also Chairman of the Fund Raising Committee of the National Association of the Blind. He became a little more active after the 1992 demolition of the Babri Masjid and the 1993 communal riots in Mumbai. He, along with his wife Saira, even started the Welfare Organisation for Relief and Care Services (WORCS) to provide relief to the riot-stricken but never really identified himself with any one party though in his heart he remained a Congressman – the proof being that he accepted a nomination to the Rajya Sabha in 2000 on a Congress ticket.

In the Rajya Sabha he gave a good account of himself making his maiden speech on a subject other than films. *The Times of India* reported that he "made an impressive debut in his new role as a Rajya Sabha member". Taking part in the discussion on drought in many states, Dilip Kumar made a strong plea for harnessing abundant water going waste.

"There is immense scope for tapping the water of rivers flowing down the mountains," he said, harking back to his tour of the Himalayas in Uttar Pradesh. It was indeed tragic that the water which was adequate enough to meet the challenge of a drought, was washing away villages and inundating crops, he added without theatrical flourishes.

Quoting experts from abroad with whom he had discussed the issue, Dilip Kumar said, "We can irrigate the whole country if this water can be tapped." Some American experts had told him that the water flowing down the Himalayas could, in fact, be exported. Getting right to the point when he rose to speak, Dilip Kumar said irrigation was the "most profound issue" for the country, and water preservation should be taken as a new national challenge.

The controversy about his accepting the Nishan-e-Imtiaz, the highest civilian award in Pakistan, seems to have permanently embittered him and though he is reconciled to it he seems to have withdrawn from public life completely, which is sad because an actor and a citizen of his statesman-like stature had so much to offer.

Chapter Eighteen

– *The Private Life of a Public Man* –

It was a scandal that shocked his fans who, in spite of his whispered misdemeanours as a star and an actor, worshipped him like a demi-God. After several months of gossip-mongering in the "smaller film magazines", the scandal finally broke in February 1982 when the *Current* weekly published the **nikahnama** which pronounced Mohammad Yusuf Khan and Asma Begum as husband and wife and gave lie to Dilip Kumar's month-long denials of "any marriage alliance to a woman named Asma". Of course, during the course of the month he had progressed from not knowing the woman at all to knowing her only socially. So this ultimate revelation was not completely unexpected to the unbiased observer.

Assiduous gossip writers discovered that Asma was a well-known Hyderabad socialite who loved the fast life: late nights parties, horse riding and racing, playing rummy and music. The romance had begun several years earlier in Hyderabad and had blossomed in the garden city of Bangalore, the beautiful Solan Hills of Himachal Pradesh, the stately Mughal environs of Delhi, to Panchgani and the Turf Club of Pune – away from the prying eyes of the Bombay *papparazi*.

The romance culminated in a secret marriage ceremony held on May 30, 1981 at a suite in Hotel West End in Bangalore. The presiding **kazi** was Maulana Hafiz Abdul Hafiz Junedi and the witnesses were Asma's uncle Amanullah Khan and her best friend and confidante Anu Verma. Everyone at the marriage ceremony was sworn to secrecy because Dilip Kumar needed some time to break the news to the world and, indeed, his first wife Saira Banu. Dilip Kumar then was being considered for the Rajya Sabha and a second marriage would have spoilt his chances.

Why then did Dilip Kumar do all this to get married a second time? Listen to Dilip Kumar's side of the story. He claimed that Asma was a family friend who he had known for eight years but met only nine times. "The last time we met a few of her friends played a trick on her and locked the two of us in a room overnight," recalled Dilip at the height of the controversy. Being the cultured people that they were, naturally, nothing untoward happened but when Asma confessed the incident to her husband, he threw her out of the house.

Feeling guilty and responsible, Dilip offered her monetary help, which was promptly refused. "So I did what a gentleman should do and married her," said Dilip. Surely a heavy price to pay for what was, after all, an innocent prank played by friends! In any case, and for some unidentifiable reason, Dilip's second wife was much more acceptable to the Khan family than the first one because the new bride was installed in Dilip Kumar's bungalow at 48, Pali Hill where the Khan family stayed. Asma wanted nothing but the one thing she must have aspired for the most: freedom. She was not permitted to leave the house without a chaperon – and that too, late at night lest the world discover Dilip Kumar's indiscretion.

It was something even Saira Banu had not suspected because in the months preceding the breaking of the scandal she had been as staunch in her denials as Dilip Kumar. Speaking to a film magazine several months later, at the height of the scandal, she confessed that the first inkling that she had about **Saab**'s indiscretion was when she heard the servants whispering about the new woman in **Saab**'s life. She confronted Dilip who, at first, denied them as mere rumours, which every film star is afflicted with. "In fact, he took the Koran and swore by it," recalls Saira. Later, when the newspapers began to give proof, he could not deny it anymore. Confessed Saira, "It was always my childhood dream to be Mrs Dilip Kumar. Today it has turned into a nightmare."

Saira really did not believe the "honourable" reason that he had given her. She was upset and said so, "How could he honour another woman and dishonour his wife?" She was also upset about the rumours, which were growing like wildfire, that Dilip had remarried in order to have children, to beget an heir. What gave further strength to these rumours was the fact that Saira had given birth to a stillborn child just a few months ago in 1981. "There is no doctor in the world who has told me that I cannot have a child," she said categorically, dismissing the rumours.

Dilip pleaded with Saira to stand by his side. "**Mujhse galti ho gayee! Kiss-se galti nahin hoti**?" he said, "If you stand by me now you will be helping me out of this sorry mess that I have got into." Saira decided she would stand by her husband and fight for him. In an interview with a film magazine she had openly declared, "I will give my life for my husband but I will never share him."

Things may have cooled down but for the fact that Asma also began to give interviews to the Press. Dilip, rightly or wrongly, had also begun to suspect that she was responsible for leaking out the **nikahnama** to put added pressure on him. What was worse! The witnesses to the marriage, Anu Verma and Amanullah Khan also began to issue Press statements, which Asma would not deny. With statements being issued to the Press from all the parties concerned, Dilip was well and truly cornered and let her know his intentions: to divorce her! This was sometime in October 1982.

The actual divorce would come through in January 1983. Between October 1982 and January 1983 Dilip Kumar is said to have visited Asma only thrice: once when she became hysterical and ran out of the house barefooted; when she allegedly took an overdose of sleeping tablets; and finally when she went on a hunger strike. And yet, Dilip refused to relent. He had made his choice: it was to be his wife of 16 years. Dilip kept pressurising Asma to sign the official papers and receive the **meher** of Rs 3 lakhs.

Finally a joint statement was issued: "We have mutually dissolved our marriage for entirely personal reasons and in view of circumstances that did not sustain congeniality, we part with the fullest regard and respect for one another and with no bitterness or rancour. We sincerely wish each other happiness in our respective lives. All the covenants of the **nikahnama** have been completed with according to Islamic tenets." The divorce officially came through on January 22, 1983 and Dilip Kumar attended the shooting of Ramesh Talwar's *Duniya* at Rajkamal Studios.

A decade later *Stardust* caught up with Asma who confided, "I don't care any more. What more do I have to lose? The things a woman lives for, her honour, her children, her love – I have none. Life has no meaning any more for me."

Saira Banu had this to say about the episode: "It's not a fairy tale any longer. I did not get children and I did not need material security. He was my emotional anchor once. Now my eyes have opened. I never see dreams in broad daylight. Marriage is only an arrangement of convenience. We are a well-adjusted couple, which is more than you can say of most."

Dilip Kumar never refers to the episode.

Chapter Nineteen

– *Putting Character in his Roles* –

There comes a time in the life of every star when he can no longer hide his true age. If he hasn't had the courage to retire before that he is forced to choose between retiring then or continuing into what are euphemistically known as character roles. More often than not these character roles are just fleeting two-bit appearances of fathers, uncles, doctors, bosses ... or whatever role that is going. Often the decision to retire or not is an economic one. More often, it is just the unwillingness to shift from centre-stage into total obscurity.

Dilip Kumar did consider retirement when he was still flush from the super successes of *Mughal-e-Azam* and *Gunga Jumna*. He was barely 40 years old then and retirement would have given him the mystique of a Garbo. The moment passed and he went on to do more films. Maybe he was right for he still had a *Ram Aur Shyam* and an *Aadmi* to show for it. Hindi cinema would surely have been poorer without these two films. But what of the others like *Dastaan* and *Bairaag*, which would have been best unmade?

Bairaag was released in 1976 and sank without a trace. No more leading roles came his way. He was obviously too old for them. For several years he sat and wondered about his next step. Films were still being offered but not the kind of roles he could be proud of. Character roles in Hindi cinema are generally of the "daddy-uncle" type and no one – not even Ashok Kumar – has escaped the ignominy of doing such roles. And then came his one-time co-star Manoj Kumar with an offer, which would give him a new direction. Recalls Manoj, "*Kranti* was the greatest chapter of my life. When I asked Dilip Kumar to work in *Kranti* he was thrilled and said that it would be a pleasure working with me. It took me just five minutes to narrate the story of *Kranti* and it took him just one minute to say yes."

Manoj Kumar found the interaction thrilling, "The man who is called a great menace, who mauls writers and directors and actors did not change a line of what I had written and did not alter a scene." Dilip did not have to because, though he was not the leading man of the film, his was the pivotal role and it was written for him. After all, Manoj Kumar may have been a questionable actor but there were few who

A triumph of characterisation...scenes from *Shakti*

can match him as writer and director – particularly in his own genre of home-brew patriotism. Besides, having handled huge star casts before, Manoj knew that he had to do justice to all the stars in his film or he would end up with a box office failure.

In a sense *Kranti* gave an indication of what Dilip Kumar would and would not do. It became clear to producers that he was willing to accept a film in which he had "something to do", where there was a clearly outlined script with his role clearly marked out. Ramesh Sippy's *Shakti*, written by Salim-Javed, pitted Dilip Kumar opposite the star of the era: Amitabh Bachchan. The film was a winner from the start. Ramesh Sippy had a rock-solid track record as a director, Salim-Javed were still at the height of their creativity, and Amitabh Bachchan was the reigning superstar and a superb actor to boot.

Shakti must have been a huge challenge for Dilip Kumar and he met it head-on. Commenting on Dilip Kumar's delineation of the role Salim Khan, one of the writers of the film, said, "We were amazed that he has given a whole new dimension to the character we had written. It happens very rarely that you have a competent script and the film goes beyond what you imagined. Dilip Kumar understood the character and enhanced it his own way."

Shakti would have been an excellent psychological portrait of a son resentful of his father who values his duty above all else. Unfortunately the compulsions of the box office are such that no writer can ignore them totally. In spite of that, there was a lot of talk about his crossing histrionic swords with Amitabh Bachchan. Commenting on the younger actor Dilip said, "Amitabh Bachchan is a complete actor in himself, a man of excellent deportment from what I've seen but I do feel he could've avoided getting stuck in a groove." This said with a straight face, quite oblivious to the fact that he as an actor had also allowed himself to be caught in the image trap.

But now Dilip Kumar was getting ready for another kind of image:

that of an honest man who turns to crime because of a crucial incident which makes him realise the futility of remaining honest. This theme has its roots in a Marathi play written by Madhusudhan Kalelkar, *Ashrunchi Jhali Phule*, remade in Hindi as *Aansoo Ban Gaye Phool* with Ashok Kumar playing the central role of the honest man-turned-criminal genius. Having played the wronged man all his life this addendum of crossing over to the other side must have appealed to the actor in him: to play the hero and the villain, both at the same time! We have seen that there had always been this desire to play negative characters.

With a few embellishments and story changes Dilip Kumar played this role in his next three films: *Vidhaata* (1983), directed by Subhash Ghai; *Mashaal* (1984), directed by Yash Chopra; and *Duniya* (1984), directed by Ramesh Talwar. The only other film he completed in between was B.R.Chopra's *Mazdoor*. Reminiscent of *Naya Daur* and *Paigham* but with an urban background, the film was a neatly directed and acted film which has not largely been noticed because of the higher profile films that Dilip Kumar was then doing. Apart from raising the issues of Labour-versus-Capital, the film focuses on a confrontation between a father (Dilip Kumar) and his foster son (Raj Babbar) and is a gem of a film worthy of greater attention.

Dilip Kumar's association with Subhash Ghai during the making of *Vidhaata* resulted in the young director signing him up for two more films: *Karma* and *Saudagar*. Though the focus of *Karma* was on its three main heroes (Anil Kapoor, Jackie Shroff and Naseeruddin Shah), Dilip Kumar had a clearly etched out character of the jailor who crosses swords with a dangerous criminal (Anupam Kher). *Saudagar* once again had Dilip Kumar crossing swords with Raaj Kumar and that, thanks to a somewhat weaker main cast (Manisha Koirala and Vivek Mushran, who were both newcomers then), became the highlight of the film. Much was made of the giants of histrionics battling it out on location in the film's pre-release publicity but the actual film seemed to be evenly balanced.

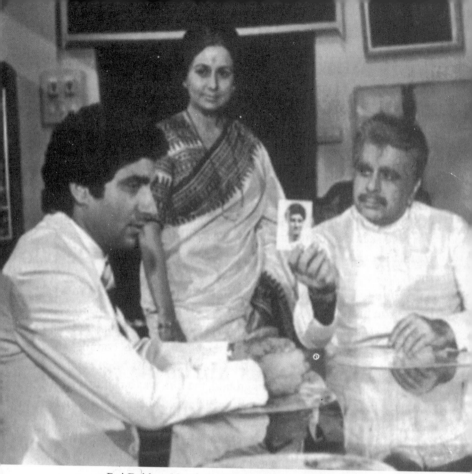

Raj Babbar, Nanda and Dilip Kumar in *Mazdoor*

Subhash Ghai is himself a strong director who will not take too kindly to interference from his actors. How then did his association with Dilip Kumar develop considering that the actor cannot keep himself away from the director's job? Says Subhash, "There have been differences of opinion but we have tried to thrash them out before going to the sets. We do our homework thoroughly which makes everything so easy. Actually, this actor called Dilip Kumar is least interested in getting involved in your job if you are good. He is totally absorbed in his own work but he cannot sit back and see work suffer because of indifference, ineptitude and insincerity. This man's professionalism, his total dedication, his integrity and his passion for work are mind-blowing."

Another surprise which Dilip Kumar had for his fans was that he could still romance at his age (sixty-plus then) and get away with it. Almost all his films of this period have a strong romantic patch and the audience loved every moment of it. Only a Dilip Kumar can get away with it because when he romances a Waheeda Rehman (*Mashaal*), Nanda (*Mazdoor*), Nutan (*Karma, Kanoon Apna Apna*) he does so with great style and lends it the credibility of lived moments.

Dilip Kumar's remaining films during this phase are best forgotten: *Dharam Adhikari* (1986), *Kanoon Apna Apna* (1989) and *Izzatdar* (1990). *Aag Ka Dariya*, though completed in 1991, was never released while *Qila* was completed in the early 1990s but was released only in 1998. Why he signed up these films will remain one of the unsolved mysteries of the cinema industry but he did have an answer for it, "Selectiveness has been my hallmark from the beginning and it is this that has enabled me to survive for so long. Today you cannot choose between good and bad films. You have to choose between bad and horrible films. So, do you blame me if I chose the bad films?"

Dilip Kumar also found it "exasperating to work with the new breed of directors". In a magazine interview he said, "I cannot say that the new style of functioning suits my temperament. Our films are also becoming like fast food and this breakneck pace is taking us nowhere. There is no time to concentrate, no atmosphere to imbibe, absorb and deliver. Which is why I decided to give up acting again." But he was willing to direct, not realising that even as director he would be subject to the same pressures of the marketplace.

The only positive aspect (if it can be called that!) of doing a film like *Izzatdar* was that the film's producer Sudhakar Bokade asked him to direct a film for him. Recalls Bokade, "This was during the making of *Izzatdar*. My director K.Bapaiah fell ill and the schedule was as good as cancelled when Dilip Kumar offered to direct that schedule. When I saw him on the sets I was mesmerised. I was impressed by his directorial style and more so, by the way in which the other artistes responded to his direction. It was after that I asked him to direct a film for me."

Seeing that his acting career was literally fading out into inconsequential films, Dilip agreed and *Kalinga* was announced. Dilip Kumar gave an indication of how the film was shaping and his

Bringing character to his roles: Clockwise –with Anil Kapoor in *Mashaal*; with Sunjay Dutt in *Vidhaata*; with director Ramesh Sippy on the sets of *Shakti*; with Anil Kapoor in *Mashaal;* in *Duniya*

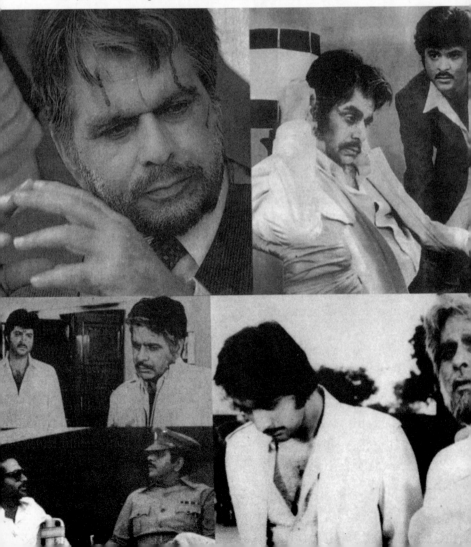

own outlook to direction, "*Kalinga* may be a bit short on buffoonery, fisticuffs and bang-bang. Ingredients finally don't count, the audience does. They should like the film, the critics too. I am certainly not starting a revolution with *Kalinga*. I expect to be assessed like any other director."

Several schedules and misunderstandings later the film ground to a halt. There was talk of another director completing the film but eventually a patchwork solution was found: Dilip Kumar would complete the film because Sudhakar Bokade still had great faith in him. But by then Bokade's own financial affairs were in a mess. His own life was under scrutiny and the film never progressed towards completion.

Dilip Kumar has not acted in a film in over a decade. And it is doubtful if he ever will now. But the restlessness to do something continues for he claims, "You have to keep growing. Stagnation means death. Each experience adds to your growth and the more you grow the more you live. I am still living and learning."

Chapter Twenty

– Pilgrimage to Peshawar –

April 2, 1988. That was the day that a 45-year-old dream came true. To return to his roots, the city which had given birth to him. The city of his forefathers and ancestors. A city which now, unfortunately, lay in another country.

Dilip Kumar, due to his immense histrionic talent, was a man who was adored not only in India but also in Pakistan, which now laid claim to the city of Peshawar where he had been born so many decades ago in 1922. And so, that made the return to his roots so much simpler.

Shouts of "Dilip Kumar zindabad! Yusuf Khan zindabad!" pierced through the Karachi sky as the plane carrying Dilip Kumar, wife Saira Banu and brother Ahsan Khan taxied on the airport runway and came to a halt. The Chief Protocol Officer of Sind was present at the airport and an official car soon whisked the guests away to the **mazar** of Quaid-e-Azam Mohammad Ali Jinnah, the architect of Pakistan.

Later in the afternoon the legendary actor and his wife were welcomed and felicitated by the Fatimid Foundation, at whose invitation the couple had come to spend two weeks in Pakistan. Refusing to answer any question on films he said, "I prefer to involve myself in social work now." That evening the couple were distinguished guests at a dinner hosted by the Chief Minister of Sind. Once again Dilip Kumar reiterated his desire "to work for the welfare of society".

The next day the trio reached Peshawar to an even more tumultuous welcome by the Mayor, Deputy Mayor and other high-ranking officials of the city. People shouting slogans had lined up on either side of the streets through which Dilip Kumar's convoy of cars passed. Dilip

Dilip Kumar and Saira Banu receiving a warm welcome in Peshawar

Kumar and his wife were seated in an open car so that his innumerable fans could catch a glimpse of the star. The convoy passed through various streets so that the guests could see the city culminating at the house of the Governor Fida Hasan Khan.

Dilip Kumar spent a week in Peshawar and naturally a visit to the house in which he was born was a must. "I thought it was a big house but it seems somewhat smaller," he said recalling the many happy days he had spent there. Peshawar was pure nostalgia for the actor who spent the entire week meeting cousins and relatives of the Peshawar branch. The Pathans of Peshawar tried to measure up the legendary actor to find out how much of a Pathan he still was after having spent his life so far away in Bombay. Dilip Kumar fantasised about what would have happened had he stayed back in Peshawar but hastily added that he would never have become Dilip Kumar, which was only possible because of Bombay and Bombay Talkies.

Another nostagic visit was to the seat of the Pakistani film industry in Lahore where he met old co-stars Swarnalata (*Pratima*) and Noorjehan (*Jugnu*). The ones he could not meet were Mumtaz Shanti (*Ghar Ki Izzat*) and Shaukat Hussein Rizvi (producer-director of *Jugnu*). And then there were old friends Mohammad Ali and Nadeem.

If nothing else the trip brought home the fact that whatever may be the boundaries that divide the sub-continent the people still admire the same stars, the same films and, indeed, the same culture.

Chapter Twenty-One

– *The Lion in Winter* –

The last decade has been a turbulent one for Dilip Kumar. The changes that have come about in the world around him and the film industry in particular have affected him deeply. As an actor he has not had a single major release. His last hyped release was Subhash Ghai's *Saudagar* in 1991, in which he crossed histrionic swords with Hindi cinema's greatest stylist Raaj Kumar. He has acted in two more films after that and directed one but none has made much of an impact. Umesh Mehra's *Qila* was released as late as 1998 and sank without a trace. The other two – *Aag Ka Dariya* and *Kalinga* – are yet to see the light of the projection lamp.

Soon after *Qila*'s delayed but limited release several other producers began to think of casting Dilip Kumar. Producer Dinesh Patel and director Kuku Kohli went ahead and announced *Asar –The Impact* which was to be a romantic thriller with thespian Dilip Kumar playing a grandfather. The film went on the floors in 2001 with the mahurat shot being taken on Priyanka Chopra and Ajay Devgan cuddling in a swimming pool. Dilip Kumar was present and even sounded the first clapperboard. However the film made no progress and was eventually scrapped sometime in 2003.

Another film which was announced with great fanfare was Tanvir Ahmed's *Ada*, also starring Amitabh Bachchan. The titans were to star together after a gap of 15 years, their last being *Shakti*. The film was to be presented by Jhamu Sugandh while A R Rahman was to compose the music. But again there was no news of the film and it was allowed to die a quiet death.

In any case ill-health has dogged Dilip Kumar in recent years. In September 2003 he was admitted to the intensive care unit of the Mumbai-based Leelavati Hospital after his blood pressure and blood sugar levels shot up due to the stress of having attended a few film functions. But that has not deterred him from attending them. As recently as April 10, 2005 he was seen at the Baburao Patel Centenary celebrations where he and his wife Saira Banu were felicitated by Mrs Sushila Rani Patel. Much earlier on October 5, 2004 he was honoured by the British Film Institute at the National Film Theatre in London with a retrospective of eleven of his best films: *Jugnu, Devdas, Deedar, Andaz, Babul, Madhumati, Gunga Jamna, Shakti, Mughal-e-Azam, Bairaag* and *Footpath*.

Announcing the festival earlier in August the NFT had said: "We are delighted to welcome Dilip Kumar to the NFT on October 5 as one of the leading lights of Hindi cinema for almost sixty years." The NFT held the season in association with a Bradford organisation, Bite the Mango, which does commendable work in bringing together Indians and Pakistanis through the medium of Hindi films. The films itself were a feast for lovers of Hindi cinema, many of them being unspooled for the first time in London. The session with the legendary actor, moderated by the noted economist and Dilip Kumar admirer Lord Meghanand Desai was also a sell-out.

He made a single foray into production nearly four decades back and though the film was a great success the experience itself was so bitter that he did not find it worth repeating. He took up direction in a bid to extend his association with cinema but the film *Kalinga* was never completed probably because the producer Sudhakar Bokade could not keep pace with Dilip Kumar's quest for perfection. The resulting skirmish between the producer and director further delayed the release of the film and Bokade landed in a financial mess which was so bad that that he spent the next seven years of his life sorting them out. "Well, that has all been sorted out. Dilip-saab and I have now become very good friends. We are planning to start the post-production of the film very soon so that we'll be able to release it some time this year," says Bokade. So, Dilip Kumar fans may yet get to see the star's name under the title of the director.

And then there is the untitled documentary on Dilip Kumar being made by Subhash Ghai who gave the thespian his biggest trilogy of blockbusters in the later years of his career – *Vidhaata, Karma* and *Saudagar*. According to Ghai the documentary will focus on the thespian's early days in Peshawar, his struggles in Mumbai, his golden career and his present days. At the moment the film is being researched meticulously. Says Subhash Ghai, "My documentary will show clippings of the maestro's movies, his comments at length and, of course, interviews of his co-stars, technicians and music director Naushad, who contributed greatly to making what Dilip Kumar is today. I will, of course, interview Mrinal Sen and Tapan Sinha and seek their comments on Dilip Kumar."

Dilip Kumar on his part says, "I will speak at length on Bimal Roy, Nitin Bose, K Asif and my beloved Tapanda. Satyajit Ray will get a special mention. Ashok Kumar and Motilal were actors who performed virtually effortlessly. My contemporaries, Raj (Kapoor) and Dev (Anand) slogged it to the top by dint of merit and hard work. My heroines, Meena Kumari, Nargis, Madhubala, Vyjayantimala and Waheeda Rehman were great performers. Of course, Talat Mehmood and Mohd Rafi lent their best voices."

One undoubted highlight of the recent years was the re-release of the digitally corrected and colourised version of *Mughal-e-Azam*. When the film had been first released on August 5, 1960, people had slept in queues for days outside ticket windows, eager to see the near-mythological lovers play out their story onscreen. This time the film was released at the same time as another major blockbuster *Veer Zaara*, directed by Yash Chopra and starring the new Badshah of Bollywood, Shah Rukh Khan and yet, it held on to its own ground. The new generation marvelled at K.Asif's imagination and the technical virtuosity of a film made 45 years ago. Dilip Kumar's histrionics once again became the talk of the town.

Talking at a recent seminar filmmaker Mahesh Bhatt said, "Recently I was told by the Ministry of Information and Broadcasting that *Mughal-E-Azam* was also screened in the Srinagar Valley, where Hindi movies have not been playing for years. The major bulk of the audience consisted of young people. Now, ever since trouble began in Kashmir, the young people of that region have been violently opposing anything 'Indian', even Hindi movies. The cinema hall where the film was now being shown was earlier forced to close shop because no one came to the hall to watch Hindi films. But *Mughal-e-Azam* shocked everybody. Not only was it running to packed houses, but all those young people who came to watch the film clapped and applauded all through it." But for all the hype that the film attracted in India, it did just average business outside the country in the Middle East, USA and UK in spite of the fact that Dilip Kumar attended the film's premiere in Dubai.

Another Dilip Kumar classic which is now being colourised and digitally restored is B.R.Chopra's *Naya Daur*. Says Ravi Chopra, "My father made classic films in black and white and we don't want them to be forgotten. Today's generations are more familiar with colour cinema and we want them to see *Naya Daur* in full glory in colour. You see, it has a lot of spectacle, like the race between the bus and the horse cart even while stressing the value of tradition. The film will retain its original 18 reels and run for about three hours." The entire process is expected to cost Rs 3 crores which is more than the cost of the original film but it is yet another chance to see Dilip Kumar in full bloom.

There was a brief period during the early 1990s at the fag end of his active acting career when Dilip Kumar seemed to be preparing himself for a public life. He then accepted to be the Chairman of the Fund Raising Committee of the National Association of the Blind. He became a little more politically active after the 1992 demolition of the Babri Masjid and the 1993 communal riots in Mumbai when he thought he needed to give voice to the woes of the common man. He, along with his wife Saira, even started the Welfare Organisation for Relief and Care Services (WORCS) to provide relief to the riot-stricken. He never really identified himself with any one communal group or party and in his heart he remained a Congressman – probably the last remnant of the Nehruvian dream.

He seemed to have reached the nadir during the controversy which centered around his accepting the Nishan-e-Imtiaz, the highest civilian award conferred on him by the Government of Pakistan. What should have been a private decision for him to make became a public debate forcing him to take a stance which was perceived as anti-national. The hurt seems to have permanently embittered him and though he is reconciled to it he seems to have withdrawn from public life completely – coming out of his shell only for a brief stint at the Rajya Sabha.

The only highpoint of the last decade for Dilip Kumar was in the year 2000 when a Congress nomination saw him in the Rajya Sabha, where he gave a good account of himself. *The Times of India* reported that he "made an impressive debut in his new role as a Rajya Sabha member", making his maiden speech on a subject other than films. Taking part in the discussion on drought in many states, Dilip Kumar made a strong plea for harnessing abundant water going waste. The paper did not bother to report any other speeches the thespian may have made.

Today, everything is quiet at 10, Pali Hill, Mumbai. The fans no longer stand outside the gates waiting for a glimpse of the elusive star. Producers no longer sit on the sofas holding tightly onto the scripts of proposed films. The world seems to have forgotten the star who gave so many hits, the actor who gave so many memorable performances, the suave urbane man who made so much of a difference to the public life of Mumbai, if not India.

Not that it matters to Dilip Kumar for he has always discouraged adulation. He has always preferred to live a very private life – submitting only to the publicity demanded by his profession. He has jealously guarded his family life against any invasion from the media and refused to share his innermost thoughts. Once, several years ago, he was asked why he did not write an autobiography and he retorted, "Some things are best left unsaid."

Even today there are many – stars and critics – who swear by his histrionics, still look upon him as a king among actors. The sad thing is that not many of them are really familiar with the films he has made – let alone seen his best performances! The sadder thing is that his truly great films are lost somewhere in the vast ocean of cinema.

But to those who have seen his films and have felt thrilled with his performances … to those who have known the man and shared his conversation … it will be impossible to forget the star, the actor or the man. As long as there is Indian cinema, Dilip Kumar's performances will be seen and discussed for he is truly an emperor among actors!

End of Book Notes 1

The Actor's Actor

When Dilip Kumar was starting out at Bombay Talkies and wasn't too sure about what he was doing, he was lucky enough to have a senior actor like Ashok Kumar around to give him acting tips and generally help him out. Once, much later, he confided to Ashok Kumar, "I really don't know what acting is all about and I am terrified that some day I may be exposed for what I am: an imposter. **Pol khul jayegi**." The veteran actor stared back at the fledgling actor and dead-panned, "Don't worry! I, too, used to feel the same way. But I haven't got caught yet! In any case, I think you, too, have managed it well. You die in every film and are so convincing as if you have really passed away."

In spite of this Dilip Kumar never really lost the feeling that he was an imposter. Talking about this feeling several decades later he confessed, "I remember being asked by the director in one scene to look terribly shocked and pained because my 'mother has just died'. (Dilip Kumar is probably talking about that immortal scene from Amiya Chakraborty's *Daag*.) And this voice inside me said: she's not your real mother, nor has she died, she's merely holding her breath for the scene. It's all pretence; so how can you pretend to be pained? And why? Is this any way to live, pretending all the time?" But slowly he learned to control such thoughts and concentrate on giving credibility to the world of make-believe.

He had admired Paul Muni and Spencer Tracy in the formative period as an actor but had become a great admirer of Marlon Brando (and thus the Stanislavsky Method) during the most creative and prolific period of his life. From them he learned to think deeply about his characters and work on his performances. He went all the way to Mahalaxmi to observe a blind beggar who could help him with a performance (*Deedar*). He spent six months learning the sitar so that he could give an authentic rendition for one song in a film (*Kohinoor*). He ran around the studio several times so as to get the right kind of breathlessness for a shot (*Daag*). But he was also the actor who refused to watch K.L.Saigal play Devdas because it would then influence his performance. In doing so he set about a style which was uniquely his own.

There were only two other actors before him – Ashok Kumar and Motilal – who set out to do what he also wanted to achieve: act naturally. "No," he says, "I faced no opposition from any of directors to my style of acting. On the contrary I was much assisted. I was given a lot of inside information and hints about how to handle myself. I learned a lot from Nitin Bose who I consider to be my mentor, friend, philosopher and guide. He taught me the need to use fewer actions, less words and still convey what you had to "by the sheer power of your expressions." And there were others: Amiya Chakraborty, Ramesh Saigal, Mehboob Khan, Bimal Roy and Hrishikesh Mukherji.

There is a story which Rishi Kapoor is fond of narrating:

R.K.Studios–Raj Kapoor was directing his younger son Rishi Kapoor for a particularly complex scene from *Prem Rog*. Rishi Kapoor was not getting it right and Raj **Saab** was getting more and more perturbed. Suddenly, from behind the camera, comes Raj **Saab**'s voice, "Chintu! Listen to me! I want Yusuf! **Mujhe Yusuf chahiye!**" Rishi did not understand what was being said. He just went from one take to another till realisation dawned on him. He submerged his own personality and played the scene the way Dilip Kumar would have played it. The scene was okayed instantly and Raj Sahab rushed forward to embrace Rishi.

Here was a great actor in his own right – one of the so-called Big Three of Hindi Cinema – and yet, here he was asking his own son to act a scene like Dilip Kumar. What could be a greater tribute to Dilip Kumar's histrionics? The incident also underscores yet another cinema reality: that Dilip Kumar has often peeped out of many an actor's performance. He has had many clones but there are a few famous ones who started as his imitators. Rajendra Kumar. Manoj Kumar. Amitabh Bachchan. Shahrukh Khan. The fact that they have managed to create identities of their own due to the sheer force of their personalities does not alter the fact. The others just fell by the wayside.

Said Rajendra Kumar, "He started a whole new school of acting and I have no hesitation in saying that I was one of his earliest followers. I know a lot of people call me a copy of Dilip Kumar and I say that I am! I am proud that I imitated the best." As Manoj Kumar, who has often been accused of imitating him, says, "Tell me which actor in the last forty years has the guts to keep his hand on his heart and say that he has not imitated or tried to imitate Dilip Kumar?"

Most of the younger actors do not even mind if they are told they are imitating Dilip – so much is the respect they hold him in. Amitabh Bachchan rates Dilip on par with Hollywood giants like Marlon Brando, and is convinced that if he was born across the seven seas he would have most definitely won several Oscars. According to Anil Kapoor, who has co-starred with Dilip Kumar in three films (*Shakti, Mashaal, Karma*), working with Dilip is a learning process. His enthusiasm and dedication for work are infectious. Jackie Shroff admits that during the making of *Ram Lakhan* he could see that Subhash Ghai was "searching for Dilip Kumar in me." Shahrukh Khan, who is often said to be the modern-day Dilip Kumar, says, "It is flattering to me but I cannot even dream of reaching the position he is in today."

If any actor escaped the label then it was undoubtedly Sanjeev Kumar who matched Dilip Kumar gesture for gesture, nuance for nuance in both *Sunghursh* and *Vidhaata*. So much so that even Dilip Kumar sat up and took notice of the actor. When asked Sanjeev Kumar retorted, "He is great and there is no doubt about it. I may have acted well but then whatever I have done has been the influence of the actor who is a school for all time, Dilip Kumar."

As an actor he has received an unprecedented eight Filmfare awards (including that one rare hat-trick in 1955/1956/1957). Even an international honour for his acting at Karlovy Vary. But never the National award. So, when he was awarded the Dadasaheb Phalke Award for Lifetime Achievement in Cinema in 1995 there was a fleeting moment when he thought he would refuse the award. "I had never received the National Award for any of my performances. I thought I was never in the reckoning. So when the Phalke award was announced I felt: 'Why now?'," he recalls his reaction to when the award was announced for the first time. But the congratulatory messages and floral tributes that started flowing in so overwhelmed the actor that he thought it would be "very small and churlish" to refuse an award which reflected "the profuse affection of the people".

End of Book Notes 2

– The Soul of an Actor –

By the 1950s Raj Kapoor ... Dev Anand ... Dilip Kumar ... had become the Big Three of Hindi Cinema, each having carved out his own domain from which to rule over the hearts of the fans. Music, too, had become an essential part of entertainment cinema and each of the "kings" had his own "in-house" composer: Raj Kapoor and Shanker-Jaikishan. Dev Anand and S D Burman. Dilip Kumar and Naushad. And though Dilip Kumar scored hits with other music directors like O P Nayyar (*Naya Daur*), Salil Chowdhury (*Madhumati*) and Shanker-Jaikishan (*Daag*), most of his blockbusters and many of his hit songs were scored by Naushad.

Equally important was the "voice" – "the soul of the actor", as Raj Kapoor called it! Before Mohammad Rafi came to be known as the voice of Dilip Kumar there was Talat Mahmood. And, before Talat, there was Mukesh. But through all this there was always a Naushad to steer Dilip through his vocal acrobatics.

Naushad underscored this creative asssociation and gave it validity by claiming: "My association with Dilip Kumar sprang essentially from the fact that this thespian brought the same dedication to his craft as I did to my art. To ensure that this dedication never got diluted, I have always worked on only one film at a time -- exactly as Dilip Kumar had done."

Though Anil Biswas was the first to use Mukesh as the voice of Dilip Kumar with a snatch of **"yaad rakhna chaand taaron iss suhani raat ko"** in *Anokha Pyar*, it was left to Naushad to use the same Mukesh more consistently for Dilip Kumar in *Mela* and *Andaz*. Mukesh then was in the firm grip of the Saigal trance. Having heard

Saigal sing **"jab dil hi toot gaya"** for the maestro in *Shahjehan* he was determined to be the second Kundan Lal Saigal. Naushad was equally determined to prove to Mukesh that he had a unique voice and that he did not need to imitate Saigal. The result was the hit music of *Mela* where Mukesh warbled tune after hit tune: **"gaaye ja geet milan ke"**, **"dharti ko aakash pukare"**, **"main bhanwara tu hai phool"** and **"mera dil todnewale"**. Mohammed Rafi had the hit solo **"yeh zindagi ke mele"**.

Naushad fine tuned this further when he got Mukesh to sing **"toote na dil toote na"**, **"hum aaj kahin dil kho baithe"**, **"tu kahe agar jeevan bhar"**, and **"jhoom jhoom ke naacho aaj"** for Dilip Kumar in *Andaz* using Rafi for the sole number (**"yun toh aapas mein"**) to be picturised on Raj Kapoor -- at a time when Raj Kapoor had already hand-picked Mukesh to be his voice in *Aag* (Ram Ganguly) and *Barsaat* (Shankar Jaikishen).

With Mukesh usurped by Raj Kapoor, for some time it was thought that Talat would become the voice of Dilip Kumar – and for a brief period he did! In fact, much later Talat said, "I was very proud to sing for him, to be called his voice." Talat Mahmood first sang for Dilip Kumar in *Aarzoo* (**"Ai dil mujhe aisi jagah le chal"**) and *Babul* (**"milte hi aankhen dil hua deewana kisika"**). Several composers used his voice on Dilip Kumar for several beautiful numbers: **"Ai mere dil kahin aur chal"** (Daag), **"seene main sulagte hain armaan"** (*Tarana*), **"yeh mera diwanapan hai"** (*Yahudi*) and **"sham-e-gham ki kasam"** (*Footpath*). So well matched was his voice that when he sang for Dilip in *Devdas*, people refused to believe that it was Talat singing. They swore it was Dilip Kumar himself in the song **"Mitva laagi yeh kaisi"**. As late as 1958 Shankar Jaikishen used Talat's voice to convey Dilip's pain in *Yahudi* (**"yeh mera diwaanapan hai"**) but then that may have been because they were not too keen to use Mukesh who was irrevocably linked to the Raj Kapoor persona by then.

It was only in the 1950s that voices became an intrinsic part of the star persona: Mukesh became Raj Kapoor's "soul" very early on in the actor's career but it was only in the mid-1950s that the Kishore Kumar for Dev Anand and Mohammad Rafi for Dilip Kumar combinations became popular.

Mohammad Rafi first sang for Dilip Kumar under the baton of Firoze Nizami as early as *Jugnu* (**"yahan badla wafaa kya"**) but it was not till he sang under Naushad's baton in *Deedar* (**"meri kahani bhulne waale tera jahaan aabaad rahe"**) that he caught the fancy of the audience. Naushad emphasized the point in a dramatic fashion when, on the sets of Amar, he placed a finger on Dilip Kumar's throat and said, "Mark my words! The only voice that fits this throat is that of Rafi." The trio of Dilip Kumar-Naushad-Mohammad Rafi blazed a sensational trail from *Deedar* (**"meri kahani bhulane wale"**) to *Sunghursh* (**"mere paironmein ghunghroo"**) marking such milestones as *Udan Khatola* (1955) with **"mohabbat kee raahon mein chalna sambhal ke"**, **"na toofaan se khelo na saaheel se khelo"** and **"o door ke musafir hum ko bhi saath le le re"** reaching its high note in *Dil Diya Dard Liya* in song after song: **"koyi saagar dil ko behlaata naheen"**, **"dilruba maine tere pyaar mein kya kya na kiya, dil diya dard liya"** and **"guzare hai aaj ishq mein hum us makaam se"**.

Though the music of *Leader, Dil Diya Dard Liya* and *Sunghursh* was a huge success, the films themselves flopped at the box office and Naushad was forced to remark, "That some of Dilip Kumar's important films with me failed in the 1964-68 phase was no fault of his or mine. Both of us, in keeping with our temperament, had given nothing less than our very best to these films too." Even the success of *Ram Aur Shyam* could not salvage the combination which had given such terrific music for two decades. Producers moved on to other composers: Kalyanji Anandji (*Bairaag*), S.D.Burman (*Sagina*) and Laxmikant Pyarelal (*Dastaan*).

Naushad never again composed for a Dilip Kumar film. But his choice of Rafi as the voice of Dilip Kumar proved fortuitous .

End of Book Notes 3

– *The Ones he did not Make* –

Gharaonda/Sangam (1964)

Soon after the stupendous success of *Andaz* the acting trio of Raj-Nargis-Dilip was the talk of the town and the cynosure of all eyes. Raj Kapoor was already an established producer-director with *Aag* and *Barsaat* to his credit ... and a dreamer! He began to dream about directing a film which would star the three of them once again. Nargis was already a part and parcel of RK Films and his friendship with Dilip Kumar dated back to their college days when they played football together – if not further back into their childhood.

He had a ready script for such a film: his writer Inder Raj Anand had written *Gharaonda* as far back as 1948 when Raj was making *Aag*. Raj Kapoor floated the proposal and asked Nargis and Dilip Kumar. At first it seemed as if the film would actually take off but then, Dilip Kumar began to have second thoughts. What would it be like to be directed by a fellow star who was also sharing the histrionic credits? Dilip was not sure that the film would do him enough justice as an actor and star.

He slowly opted out and the script lay in the RK Archives till, fifteen years later, Raj, searching for a subject for his first colour film, discovered it and cast Rajendra Kumar and Vyjayanthimala to play the roles Dilip Kumar and Nargis would have played. The film was *Sangam* and it proved to be major hit!

Baiju Bawara (1952)

By the time *Baiju Bawra* was being planned Dilip Kumar was already a major star. Films like *Mela, Andaz, Babul, Jogan* and *Deedar* had ensured a certain star shine to the Dilip Kumar-Nargis pairing and though the two were never romantically linked off-screen their screen chemistry had audiences queuing up at the box office. Vijay Bhatt was · also a major producer but he preferred to make films with newcomers who would then become stars. But for *Baiju Bawra* he did think of signing Dilip Kumar and Nargis. In fact, Nargis had already been committed for Rs 50,000 with an advance of Rs 10,000 being paid to her.

Dilip Kumar was approached and he quoted a price of Rs 1.5 lakhs – an astronomical figure for the conservative Bhatts. During the conversation Dilip said that he was willing to reduce this price to Rs 1.25 lakhs. Even that was too much for the Bhatts. The meeting broke up with promises to meet again and reconsider the matter.

While the matter was still under consideration by Vijaybhai, Nargis fell ill and returned the advance given to her saying that she would not be able to do the film. Meena Kumari, who had been introduced as a child artiste by Vijaybhai's company Prakash Pictures in *Ek Hi Bhool*, agreed to do the role and was signed up for Rs 20,000. A friend introduced Bharat Bhushan to Vijay Bhatt, who felt he was ideal for the role. Bharat Bhushan was signed up for Rs 6000. Naushad who had already been signed for the music was fine with the casting. Vijay Bhatt told him, "We will work hard and make a good film. If the film turns out to be hit with Dilip and Nargis the credit will go them. If we can make a hit film without them it will be to our credit."

Both the film and its music have become landmarks in Indian film history.

Pyaasa (1957)

Dilip Kumar was by then the undisputed Tragedy King. *Andaz* had won for him the sobriquet which had been further consolidated with the release of *Devdas* and a host of films in-between. The *Pyaasa* story was tailor-made for Dilip Kumar and even Guru Dutt was very keen that he play the role. Dilip's former senior at Bombay Talkies, S.Guruswamy, who was by then Guru Dutt's right-hand man, was sent to Dilip Kumar with the script and offer.

Guru Dutt was also willing to pay any price to rope in Dilip for the role. But apparently it was not the money. During the negotiations it transpired that Dilip was not too happy with the script. He also had his reservations about playing the *Devdas* role all over again. The upshot of it was that Dilip refused the role. Guru Dutt was reluctant to offer it to any other actor and so, ended up playing it himself. *Pyaasa* went on to become one of the biggest hits of the year. More than that! Almost two decades later it acquired the status of a cult film in the world festival circuit.

Mother India (1957)

Though Mehboob Khan had expressed an initial aversion to Dilip Kumar very early on the latter's career, he was quick to revise his opinion after seeing the actor's early efforts. And once he had signed him for the landmark film *Andaz* he knew that Dilip could deliver the goods as an actor in any film. He made *Aan* and *Amar* in quick succession with Dilip Kumar playing the lead and though *Amar* was a bit of a lesser effort it was not really Dilip Kumar's fault.

So it was but natural to consider Dilip Kumar to play the lead for his next venture *Mother India*, a remake of his 1940 film *Aurat,* starring his wife Sardar Akhtar. Dilip Kumar was, of course, eyeing the meatier role of Birju, the bad son. He also convinced Mehboob that the title *This Land Of Mine* would be a much better title than *Mother India* and so, when the **mahurat** of the film was performed at Mehboob Studios in Bandra on January 7, 1955 that was the title used in the press publicity. Contrary to popular gossip, Nargis was never in the first casting of the film since *Film India* wrote, "Mehboob is still searching for a suitable girl to play the heroine and also look like Dilip Kumar's mother." But Dilip was very much a part of the initial casting for the same write-up goes on to say, "Dilip has a role after his heart and unlike the usual ones he plays."

As Dilip got more and more interested in the role, the script for *This Land of Mine* began to grow. As had happened in the case of *Amar*, Dilip began to interfere in the scripting suggesting that the film revolve around the bad son Birju. Mehboob was too much of a filmmaker to allow anyone to distort his film. He insisted that it was a "woman's picture" and that the film had to revolve around the peasant woman and her two sons. Mehboob also realised that only Nargis could do full justice to the role. Dilip suggested other actresses and even had a few of them screen-tested but once the thought had come into Mehboob's mind, Nargis it was! Once Nargis walked into the proposal there was no way she would agree to Dilip Kumar playing her son. After all, they had played screen lovers in several hit films. Who would accept them as mother and son?

Dilip Kumar never worked with Mehboob Khan again!

Lawrence of Arabia

Dilip Kumar fans would have loved to see the great actor in at least one Hollywood production but it was not to be. Dilip Kumar was only too conscious of his value in the Indian market to fritter it away playing small inconsequential roles in Hollywood films merely to impress his Indian fans. So when David Lean offered him the smaller role (eventually played by Omar Sharif) in *Lawrence of Arabia*, Dilip fended him off saying that he would rather play the title role for which Peter O'Toole had already been signed.

To cast an Asian actor (whatever his following in his home country) was a commercially impossible decision which no Hollywood producer, least of all an established one like David Lean, would take. India and crossover films were not yet in fashion as they are today. And Dilip Kumar knew that! Deep down in his heart Dilip was probably afraid that he would not be able to dictate the shaping of the script (as he had now grown used to doing) and thus, have any control over the presentation of his character in the film.

Dilip also refused the lead role in Sir Alexander Korda's dream film *Taj Mahal*. As he remarked after these refusals, "In your own bazaar you enjoy a certain status. What's the point of venturing out into fields unknown where you have no say? No contact with the subject matter."

End of Book Notes 4

– *Dilip Kumar ko Gussa Kyon aata hai?* –

Till the 1960s hardly anyone knew about the man behind the name of Dilip Kumar. Of course, in a vague sort of a way, his fans knew that his real name was Yusuf Khan and that he came of Pathan stock from the North West Frontier province of Peshawar. Indeed, several magazine articles had revealed the real name of the man and there was no secret about it. There was thus no question about hiding behind a name for it was a screen name like any other screen name that an entertainer may take for convenience. The fact that Dilip Kumar was really Yusuf Khan did not matter to anyone. He was a fine accomplished actor who was the pride of India just as an Ustad Vilayat Khan or a Bismillah Khan.

Many Muslims in the immediate post Partition period changed their names because they thought a Muslim identity would not help them get ahead in India. Dilip, however, does not see his change of name as a crisis of Muslim identity. Commenting on why he agreed to a change of name when he made his debut he says, "I changed my name because I needed a disguise. My father was strongly opposed to the idea of my becoming an actor so I thought a change of name would be prudent."

The fact that Dilip Kumar was as secular and God-fearing as the next Indian is borne out by a story, which was often narrated by Premji, who was then Production Controller of Bimal Roy Productions. Dilip Kumar was then shooting for *Madhumati* in Nainital and it was thus Premji's job to ensure his comfort. One day a priest approached Dilip Kumar and asked for help to repair a temple. Dilip called for Premji and asked him to pay the priest Rs 1000. A few days later, a **maulvi** came to Dilip with a similar request, to repair a mosque. Dilip promptly asked Premji to hand him Rs 1000. A thousand rupees was a huge amount in those days so Premji privately told Dilip to be careful about donating money. To which Dilip merely smiled and tilted his head upwards to indicate that whether it was Bhagwan or Allah they were the same to him.

As the columnist Vir Sanghvi wrote, "If you want an example of the success of Indian secularism, Dilip Kumar should fit the bill. He has been a truly patriotic Muslim. And India, in turn, has honoured him by treating him as a legend in his own lifetime. But of course, things are not that simple. No matter how successful he has been, Dilip Kumar has never been allowed to forget that he is a Muslim." The first blow came in the mid-1960s when first-time producer Dilip Kumar ran into censor trouble with *Gunga Jumna*.

The censors had raised several objections to the film, the principal one being to the last words of the dying Ganga: "Hey Ram!" Dilip Kumar did not understand the objection. After all, they were Gandhi's last words ... words which any Hindu would automatically utter in his dying moments. "Yes! Any Hindu would ...," said the man and in the silence that followed volumes were said. Of course, the film was passed after the then Prime Minister Pandit Jawaharlal Nehru intervened but Dilip never forgot the unspoken slight. But forgive it he did because he continued to be on the forefront of any national cause ... be it collecting funds for a foreign aggression or entertaining the **jawans** on the front.

Matters were further soured when, again in the early 1960s, the Bengal Police raided Dilip Kumar's house and nearly arrested him for being a Pakistani spy. The evidence against him was "the confession" of a young boy, an illegal migrant from East Pakistan (now Bangla Desh), who had worked in the houses of Bimal Roy, then Dilip Kumar and finally in the unit of Mehboob Khan. The boy had been thrown out from three houses and had finally made his way to Calcutta where he had falen in love with the daughter of a city magistrate. The magistrate had complained against the boy who was eventually arrested with the girl.

Under intensive third degree the boy had "confessed" that he was a Pakistani spy and that he was being helped by Bimal Roy, Dilip Kumar and Mehboob Khan. Eager to crack the case the Bengal Police obtained all the required permissions from the Home Ministry to raid the homes of the three film people. The fact that Dilip Kumar was a well-established film star who would hardly jeopardise his own safety and future did not matter at all! The matter dragged on for months during which all manner of rumour found tongue in Bombay till the whole matter died a quiet death for want of evidence. Once again, Dilip Kumar forgot the matter and went on with his life.

In the 1990s, particularly after the bomb blasts in Mumbai in 1993, there have always been controversies surrounding Dilip Kumar. There were even snide remarks about a trip to Dubai just before the bomb blasts. Dilip Kumar countered, "Does a trip to Dubai relate directly to the bomb blasts and Dawood Ibrahim? I had gone there in March 1993 to accompany a film delegation which was to play a cricket match for charity. I didn't go there alone. Several other artistes also went with me." Then again he was criticised for attending the Pakistan Republic Day function when he was actually at an Indian film industry reception to the Chief Secretary of the I&B Ministry.

Why doesn't Dilip Kumar ever confront these rumour-mongers? Dilip says, "I really don't understand why people are after me. What have I done? I feel so humiliated, so helpless. At this age, why am I being questioned about my credentials? My reputation, my name, my worth, everything is at stake today. You tell me how do I fight my case? I cannot go to every single person and say, Bhai! I am innocent!" The sad thing is that his credibility is at stake because he has been caught lying in public once – during the Asma case. But that was an entirely personal matter!

Dilip Kumar has always been a Congressman all his life – even having canvassed for the avowedly secular party more often than once. Probably the only time he took an openly partisan stand to support the minority Muslim community was when he spoke at the All-India Muslim OBCs Conference held in Lucknow in 1997. But that was a temporary phase, maybe caused due to some frustration with the environment, for he was back with the Congress very soon.

But all this is nothing compared to the uproar that was raised when Dilip Kumar was conferred the Nishan-e-Imtiaz, the highest civilian award given by Pakistan. On the forefront of the protest was the Shiv Sena. A couple of years before the event he had given the party a clean chit, saying, "Our grave apprehensions seem to have been laid to rest. Since the present government has come to power, the Sena, in particular, seems to be more even-handed and thoughtful. They are prepared to listen." But there were other high profile persons who joined the fray. One was industrialist Raunaq Singh who said, "You have been enjoying all the good things in India for the last 50 years or so and enjoying the love and affection of Indians as a film actor, getting all the prestigious awards. And now you suddenly turn around and say that you love Pakistan because you were born in Peshawar?"

Answering the nation which had been clamouring for him to "reject the award from an enemy nation", Dilip Kumar had this to say, "The Nishan-e-Imtiaz Award has nothing to do with politics. In an era of internationalisation and universalism, one should try to learn to co-exist with each other rather than engineer practical differences. India and Pakistan should live in peace and friendship as people of both the countries want peace." In order to diffuse the tension he appealed to the then Prime Minister Atal Bihari Vajpayee and asked him what he should do. Diplomatically Vajpayee left the decision to his conscience.

Is it something to do with the fact that he is a Muslim? After all, there were no doubts cast on Morarji Desai when he was conferred the same award in 1990. Commenting on the vilification campaign, Dilip says, "Despite the gross accusations, Dilip Kumar continues to survive. With God's grace he enjoys a great measure of the people's goodwill and affection. But this was not just thrown in his lap, he earned it the hard way. It called for investment, not of labour alone but of loyalty and care for the people I have sought to serve. I am rich inside, strong and unafraid. Untouched by the vilification targeted at me. I have tried not to nurse any bitterness because bitterness is futile."

Dilip Kumar did go to Pakistan in March 1998 to collect the award from Pakistan President Rafiq Tarar at a graceful ceremony at the Aiwan-e-Sadr (Presidency) on the occasion of Pakistan Day. Once there he discovered there were large sections of people in Pakistan who did not like the award being given to an Indian. He was charged with being a traitor who had adopted a Hindu name and preferred to remain in India. There were even some open threats like the one from Islami Jamiat-e-Talaba which said, "He should protect himself as we shall not tolerate this." But there were others like film star Mohammad Ali who said, "There ought to be no politics and no borders in the field of entertainment and this fact was borne out by the big welcome accorded to Dilip Kumar and Saira Banu." Dilip Kumar publicly proclaimed that he was accepting the award on behalf of the people of India. Back home in India he tried to bring home the fact that the common people on both sides of the border wanted peace and friendship but no one was listening.

Today, he is comfortable in his identity as an Indian Muslim. He says: "It is an identity given to him (the Indian Muslim). Personally speaking, I am comfortable with it. I am an Indian and indeed a Muslim just as my friends Subhash Ghai and Yash Chopra are Hindus and proud fellow Indians. Are people any less Indians for bearing different religious identities? It is so absurd to even think of that."

End of Book Notes 5

– Filmography –

Note: The name of the character Dilip Kumar plays in the film is given after his name in brackets.

JWAR BHATA (1944/B&W/120 minutes)
Banner: Bombay Talkies
Director: Amiya Chakraborty
Music Composer: Anil Biswas
Cast: Dilip Kumar (**Jagdish**), Mridula, Shamim, Agha Jan, K. N. Singh, Pithawala, Arun Kumar, Khalil, Bikram Kapoor & Mumtaz Ali

PRATIMA (1945B&W)
Banner: Bombay Talkies
Director: P. Jairaj
Music Composer: Arun Kumar
Cast: Dilip Kumar, Swarnalata, Jyoti, Mumtaz Ali, Pithawala, Mukri, Zebu & Shah Nawaz

MILAN (1946/B&W/144 minutes)
Banner: Bombay Talkies
Director: Nitin Bose
Music Composer: Anil Biswas
Cast: Dilip Kumar (**Ramesh**), Meera Mishra, Ranjana, Pahari Sanyal & Moni Chatterji

JUGNU (1947/B&W/148 minutes)
Banner: Shaukat Art Productions
Director: Syed Shaukat Hussein Rizvi
Music Composer: Feroz Nizami

Cast: Noorjehan, Dilip Kumar, Gulam Mohammed, Sulochana Sr. (Ruby Myers), Latika, Zia, Jilloo, Agha, Shashikala & Mohd. Rafi

ANOKHA PYAR (1948/B&W)
Banner: Ambika Films
Director: M.I.Dharamsey
Music Composer: Anil Biswas
Cast: Dilip Kumar (**Ashok**), Nargis, Nalini Jaywant, Sankatha Prasad, Mukri, Ved, Kesarbai, Uma Dutt, Habib & Sheikh

GHAR KI IZZAT (1948/B&W/136 minutes)
Banner: Murli Movietone
Director: Ram Daryani
Music Composer: Gobindram
Cast: Dilip Kumar (**Chanda**), Mumtaz Shanti, Jeevan, Manorama, Dixit, Suleman, Gulab & Gope

MELA (1948/B&W)
Banner: Wadia Films Ltd.
Director: S.U.Sunny
Music Composer: Naushad
Cast: Dilip Kumar (**Mohan**), Nargis, Jeevan, Amar, Roop Kamal, Alauddin, Abbas, Noorjehan, Chandabai, Rehman, Khalil & Baby Zubeida

NADIYA KE PAAR (1948/B&W)
Banner: Filmistan
Director: Kishore Sahu
Music Composer: C.Ramchandra
Cast: Dilip Kumar, Kamini Kaushal, Maya Banerji, David, S. L. Puri, Hari Shivdasani, Samson, Tiwari, Kanta Kumari & Ranibala

SHAHEED (1948/B&W/164 minutes)
Banner: Filmistan
Director: Ramesh Saigal
Music Composer: Ghulam Haider
Cast: Dilip Kumar (**Ram**), Kamini Kaushal, Chandra Mohan, Leela Chitnis, V. H. Desai, Shashi Kapoor

ANDAZ (1949/B&W/148 minutes)
Banner: Mehboob Productions
Director: Mehboob Khan
Music Composer: Naushad
Cast: Dilip Kumar (**Dilip**), Raj Kapoor, Nargis, V. H. Desai, Cuckoo, Murad, Anwari Bai, Amir Banu, Jamshedji, Abbas & Wasker

SHABNAM (1949/B&W/154 minutes)
Banner: Filmistan
Director: Bibhuti Mitra
Music Composer: S.D.Burman
Cast: Dilip Kumar (**Manoj**), Kamini Kaushal, Jeevan, Paro Mubarak, Haroon, Rajender Singh, Shyama and Cuckoo

ARZOO (1950/B&W)
Banner: Indian National Pictures
Director: Shaheed Lateef
Music Composer: Anil Biswas
Cast: Dilip Kumar, Kamini Kaushal, Gope, Cuckoo, Arif, Prem Dhawan, Shashikala, Sita Bose, Neelam, Khan, Ganju & Chandabai

BABUL (1950/B&W/142 minutes)
Banner: Sunny Art Productions
Director: S.U.Sunny
Music Composer: Naushad
Cast: Dilip Kumar (**Ashok**), Nargis, Munnawar Sultana, Amar, A. Shah & Jankidas

JOGAN (1950/B&W/116 minutes)
Banner: Ranjit Movietone
Director: Kidar Sharma
Music Composer: Bulo C.Rani
Cast: Dilip Kumar (**Vijay**), Nargis, Manju, Pratima Devi, Pesi Patel, Purnima, Baby Tabassum, Anwari, Ramesh Thakur, Darpan & Rajendra Kumar

DEEDAAR (1951/B&W/129 minutes)
Banner: Filmkar Limited
Director: Nitin Bose
Music Composer: Naushad
Cast: Ashok Kumar, Nargis, Dilip Kumar (**Shamu**), Nimmi, Yakub, Baby Tabassum

HULCHUL (1951/B&W)
Banner: K.Asif Productions
Director: S.K.Ojha
Music Composer: Mohd. Shafi & Sajjad Hussein
Cast: Dilip Kumar (**Kishore**), Nargis, Balraj Sahni, Yakub, Jeevan, Sitara Devi, K. N. Singh, Geeta Nizami Faizee, & Cuckoo

TARANA (1951/B&W)
Banner: Krishin Movietone
Director: Ram Daryani
Music Composer: Anil Biswas
Cast: Dilip Kumar (**Motilal**), Madhubala, Shyama, Kumar, Jeevan, Gope, Gulab, Devaskar & Bikram Kapoor

AAN (1952/B&W162 minutes)
Banner: Mehboob Productions
Director: Mehboob Khan
Music Composer: Naushad
Cast: Dilip Kumar (**Jai Tilak**), Nimmi, Premnath, Mukri, Sheela

Naik, Murad, Cuckoo, Nilam Bai, Amir Banu, & introducing Nadira.

DAAG (1952/B&W/149 minutes)
Banner: Mars & Movies
Director: Amiya Chakraborty
Music Composer: Shankar-Jaikishen
Cast: Dilip Kumar (**Shankar**), Usha Kiron, Nimmi, Lalita Pawar, Kanhaiyalal, Jawahar Kaul, Leela Mishra, Chandrashekhar & Krishnakant

SANGDIL (1952/B&W)
Banner: Talwar Films Limited
Director: R.C.Talwar
Music Composer: Sajjad Hussein
Cast: Dilip Kumar (**Shankar**), Madhubala, Leela Chitnis, Pratima Devi & Shammi

FOOTPATH (1953/B&W/148 minutes)
Banner: Ranjit Movietone
Director: Zia Sarhadi
Music Composer: Khayyam
Cast: Dilip Kumar (**Noshu**), Meena Kumari, Kuldip Kaur, Anwar Hussain, Ramesh Thapar, Achla Sachdev, Ramesh Thakur, Akhtar, P. Kailash, Jankidas, Maruti & Sumati Lajmi

SHIKAST (1953/B&W)
Banner: Asha Deep
Director: Ramesh Saigal
Music Composer: Shankar Jaikishen
Cast: Dilip Kumar, Nalini Jaywant, Master Kapoor, Om Prakash, Durga Khote, K. N. Singh, Leela Mishra, Shamlal & Hemavati

AMAR (1954/B&W/144 minutes)
Banner: Mehboob Productions

Director: Mehboob Khan
Music Composer: Naushad
Cast: Dilip Kumar (**Amarnath**), Madhubala, Nimmi, Jayant, Ullhas, Mukri, Amar, Husnbanu, Murad & Shakil Nomani

AZAAD (1955/B&W/163 minutes)
Banner: Pakshiraja Studios
Director: S.M.S.Naidu
Music Composer: C.Ramchandra
Cast: Dilip Kumar (**Azaad/Khan Saheb**), Meena Kumari, Pran, Om Prakash, S. Nazir, Badri Prasad, Raj Mehra, Randhir, Achla Sachdev, Murad, Deepa Sai, Subbalaxmi & Shammi

INSANIYAT (1955/B&W/185 minutes)
Banner: Gemini Pictures
Director: S.S.Vasan
Music Composer: C.Ramchandra
Cast: Dilip Kumar (**Mangal**), Dev Anand, Bina Rai, Vijayalaxmi, Jairaj, Jayant, Shobhana Samarth, Agha, Kumar, Badri Prasad, Mohana, Ishwarlal & Zippy, the chimpanzee.

URAN KHATOLA (1955/B&W/151 minutes)
Banner: Sunny Art Productions
Director: S.U.Sunny
Music Composer: Naushad
Cast: Dilip Kumar (**Kashi**), Nimmi, Surya Kumari, Jeevan, Agha, Nawab, Roopmala, Amar & Tun Tun
Note: The film was so successful that it was also dubbed into Tamil and shown under the name of *Vanaratham.*

DEVDAS (1956/B&W/159 minutes)
Banner: Bimal Roy Productions
Director: Bimal Roy
Music Composer: S.D.Burman
Cast: Dilip Kumar (**Devdas**), Suchitra Sen, Vyjayanthimala, Motilal, Johnny Walker, Nazir Hussein & Pran

NAYA DAUR (1957/B&W/173 minutes)
Banner: B.R.Films
Director: B.R.Chopra
Music Composer: O.P.Nayyar
Cast: Dilip Kumar (**Shankar**), Vyjayanthimala, Ajit, Chand Usmani, Jeevan, Manmohan Krishna, Nazir Hussain, Leela Chitnis, Radhakrishan, S. Nazir, Pratima Devi, Daisy Irani, S. N. Banerji & Johnny Walker

MUSAFIR (1957/B&W/149 minutes)
Banner: Film Group
Director: Hrishikesh Mukherjee
Music Composer: Salil Choudhury
Cast: Dilip Kumar (no name), Usha Kiran, Kishore Kumar, Suchitra Sen, Nirupa Roy, Shekhar, Durga Khote, David, Daisy Irani, Bipin Gupta, Rashid Khan, Nazir Hussain, Raj Laxmi, Mohan Choti, Keshto Mukherjee, Paul Mahendra & Heera Sawant

MADHUMATI (1958/B&W/179 minutes)
Banner: Bimal Roy Productions
Director: Bimal Roy
Music Composer: Salil Choudhury
Cast: Dilip Kumar (**Anand/Deven**), Vyjayanthimala, Pran, Johnny Walker, Jayant, Tarun Bose, Tiwari, Misra, Baij Sharma & Bhudo Advani

YAHUDI (1958/B&W/170 minutes)
Banner: Bombay Films
Director: Bimal Roy
Music Composer: Shanker-Jaikishen
Cast: Dilip Kumar (**Prince Marcus**), Sohrab Modi, Meena Kumari, Nigar Sultana, Nazir Hussain, Murad, Anwar, Minoo Mumtaz, Tiwari, Baby Naaz, Bikram Kapoor, Romi, Cuckoo, Kamla Laxman & Helen

PAIGHAM (1959/B&W/188 minutes)
Banner: Gemini Pictures
Director: S.S.Vasan
Music Composer: C. Ramchandra
Cast: Dilip Kumar (**Ratanlal**), Vyjayanthimala, Raaj Kumar, B. Saroja Devi, Motilal, Pandari Bai, Johnny Walker, Minoo Mumtaz, Vasundhara, David, Pratima Devi, Banerji, Shivraj, Ishwarlal & Amar

KOHINOOR (1960/B&W)
Banner: Republic Film Corporation
Director: S.U.Sunny
Music Composer: Naushad
Cast: Dilip Kumar, Meena Kumari, Jeevan, Kumkum, Mukri, Kumar, Leela Chitnis, S. Nazir, Wasi Khan, Azim, Master Nissar, Tuntun & Rajen Kapoor

MUGHAL-E-AZAM (1960/B&W/197 minutes)
Banner: Sterling Investment Corporation
Director: K.Asif
Music Composer: Naushad
Cast: Prithviraj Kapoor, Dilip Kumar (**Prince Salim**), Madhubala, Durga Khote, Nigar Sultana, Ajit, Kumar, Murad, Sheila Dalaya, Jalal Agha, Vijayalaxmi, S. Nazir, Paul Sharma, Surendra, Johnny Walker & Tabassum
Note: A digitally restored and colourised version with Dolby sound was released in November 2004.

GUNGA JUMNA (1961/Colour/178 minutes)
Banner: Citizen Films
Director: Nitin Bose
Music Composer: Naushad
Cast: Dilip Kumar (**Gunga**), Vyjayanthimala, Nasir Khan, Azra, Kanhaiyalal, Anwar, Nazir Hussain, S. Nazir, Leela Chitnis, Praveen Paul, Helen, Akashdeep, Baby Aruna & Baby Naaz

Note: Dilip Kumar's first and only foray into production. The experience so embittered him that he refused to make any more films. It is also his first film in colour.

LEADER (1964/Colour/176 minutes)
Banner: Mukerji Film Syndicate
Director: Ram Mukherji
Music Composer: Naushad
Cast: Dilip Kumar (**Vijay Khanna**), Vyjayanthimala, Motilal, Jayant, Nazir Hussain, Sapru, Hiralal, Amar, Jankidas, P. Kailash, Jagdish Sethi, Leela Misra, Merlyn & Madhumati

DIL DIYA DARD LIYA (1966/Colour/169 minutes)
Banner: Kay Productions
Director: A.R.Kardar
Music Composer: Naushad
Cast: Dilip Kumar (**Shankar**), Waheeda Rehman, Pran, Rehman, Shyama, Rani, Sajjan, Sapru, Shah Agha, Murad & Johnny Walker

WATAN KI PUKAR (1967/short film)
Banner: Mehboob Productions
Director: Mehboob
Music Composer:
Note: This was a short film on the Indo-Pak war of 1967. Dilip Kumar participated in the picturisation of the first stanza of the song, *'Awaz do, hum ek hain'*. The second and third stanzas were picturised on Raaj Kumar and Feroz Khan.

RAM AUR SHYAM (1967/Colour/171 minutes)
Banner: Vijaya International
Director: Chanakya
Music Composer: Naushad
Cast: Dilip Kumar (double roles of **Ram** and **Shyam**), Waheeda

Rehman, Mumtaz, Pran, Nirupa Roy, Kanhaiyalal, Nazir Hussain, Sajjan, Mukri, Amar, Leela Misra, Zebunissa & Baby Farida

PAARI (1967/Bengali)
Banner: Pronoti Ghosh-Bhattacharya
Director: Jayanath Chatterji
Music Composer:
Cast: Dharmendra, Dilip Kumar and Pronoti Ghosh

AADMI (1968/Colour/175 minutes)
Banner: S.V.Films
Director: A.Bhim Singh
Music Composer: Naushad
Cast: Dilip Kumar (**Rajesh aka Raja Sahab**), Waheeda Rehman, Manoj Kumar, Simi Garewal, Pran, Sulochana, Ullhas, Padma Chavan, Mohan Choti, Shivraj & Agha

SUNGHURSH (1968/Colour/158 minutes)
Banner: Rahul Theatres
Director: H.S.Rawail
Music Composer: Naushad
Cast: Dilip Kumar (**Kundan aka Bajrangi**), Vyjayanthimala, Balraj Sahni, Sanjeev Kumar, Jayant, Durga Khote, Sulochana, Sunder, Ullhas, Iftekhar, Sapru, Mumtaz Begum, Padma, Lata Sinha, Anju Mahendru, Ranu & Deven Varma

SADHU AUR SHAITAN (1968/Colour)
Banner: Bhim Singh-Mehmood Productions
Director: A.Bhim Singh
Music Composer: Laxmikant Pyarelal
Cast: Mehmood, Bharati, Kishore Kumar, Om Prakash, Pran, Baby Farida, Mukri, Manju, Raj Kishore, Keshto Mukherji, Tuntun, Jankidas, & Dilip Kumar (in a guest appearance)

GOPI (1970/Colour)
Banner: Prosperity Pictures / T. S. Muthuswamy & S. S. Palaniappan
Director: A. Bhim Singh
Music Composer: Kalyanji Anandji
Cast: Dilip Kumar (**Gopiram**), Saira Banu, Om Prakash, Pran, Johnny Walker, Lalita Pawar, Nirupa Roy, Farida Jalal, Sudesh Kumar, Durga Khote, Mukri, Tiwari, Shyamlal & Aruna Irani

SAGINA MAHATO (1970/Bengali/Colour/148 minutes)
Banner: Hemen Ganguly & J.K.Kapur
Director: Tapan Sinha
Music Composer: S.D.Burman
Cast: Dilip Kumar (**Sagina Mahato**), Saira Banu, Anil Chatterji, Kalyan Chatterji

ANOKHA MILAN (1972/Colour)
Banner: Vazirani Movies
Director: Jagannath Chatterji
Music Composer: Salil Choudhury
Cast: Dharmendra, Dilip Kumar (in a guest appearance), Pronoti Ghosh, Abhi Bhattcharya, Dilip Roy & Keshto Mukherji
Note: The film was a remake of the Bengali film *Paari*

DASTAAN (1972/Colour)
Banner: B.R.Films
Director: B.R.Chopra
Music Composer: Laxmikant Pyarelal
Cast: Dilip Kumar (double role as **Anil** and **Sunil**), Sharmila Tagore, Prem Chopra, Bindu, I. S. Johar, Padma Khanna, Madan Puri, Jayshree T., Nana Palsikar, Manmohan Krishna, Iftekar, Badri Prasad & Keshav Rana
Note: The film is a remake B.R.Chopra's earlier film Afsana (1950) for which Dilip Kumar was approached but he suggested the name of Ashok Kumar who eventually played the role.

PHIR KAB MILOGI (1974/Colour)
Banner: Shivalay Films
Director: Hrishikesh Mukherjee
Music Composer: R.D.Burman
Cast: Mala Sinha, Biswajeet, Deven Varma, Bipin Gupta, David & Dilip Kumar (in a guest appearance as **Teja Singh**)

SAGINA (1974/Hindi/Colour/148 minutes)
Banner: Rupashree International
Director: Tapan Sinha
Music Composer: S.D.Burman
Cast: Dilip Kumar (**Sagina**), Saira Banu, Om Prakash, Aparna Sen, Anil Chatterji, Swaroop Dutt, Rajni Gupta, K. N. Singh & Kader Khan
Note: The film is a remake of the Bengali film **Sagina Mahato**.

BAIRAAG (1976/Colour/141 minutes)
Banner: M. R. Productions
Director: Asit Sen
Music Composer: Kalyanji Anandji
Cast: Dilip Kumar (**triple role**), Saira Banu, Leena Chandavarkar, Prem Chopra, Nasir Khan, Helen, Nazir Hussain, Jairaj, Madan Puri, Sujit Kumar, Purnima, Asit Sen, Leela Misra, Mukri, Kadar Khan, V. Gopal, Naaz, Paintal, Jankidas, Praveen Paul, Mohan Choti & Sachin
Note: This was brother Nasir Khan's last film as an actor. It was also Kader Khan's first film. Dilip Kumar had been so impressed with Kader Khan's stage performances that he asked this engineering instructor to play a role in the film. This is also Dilip Kumar's last film as the conventional leading man.

KRANTI (1981/Colour/187 minutes)
Banner: VIP Films
Director: Manoj Kumar
Music Composer: Laxmikant Pyarelal

Cast: Dilip Kumar (**Sanga aka Kranti**), Manoj Kumar, Hema Malini, Shashi Kapoor, Parveen Babi, Shatrughan Sinha, Nirupa Roy, Shashikala, Sarika, Prem Chopra, Pradeep Kumar, Master Aditya & Master Kunal

Note: This is Dilip Kumar's first film as a character actor.

SHAKTI (1982/Colour/167 minutes)
Banner: M.R.Productions
Director: Ramesh Sippy
Music Composer: R.D.Burman
Cast: Dilip Kumar (**DCP Ashwini Kumar**), Amitabh Bachchan, Rakhee, Smita Patil, Kulbhushan Kharbanda & Amrish Puri

VIDHAATA (1982/Colour)
Banner: Trimurti Films
Director: Subhash Ghai
Music Composer: Kalyanji Anandji
Cast: Dilip Kumar (**Shamsher Singh aka Sobhraj**), Sanjeev Kumar, Shammi Kapoor, Sanjay Dutt, Padmini Kolhapure, Sarika, Amrish Puri, Shreeram Lagu, Suresh Oberoi & Madan Puri

MAZDOOR (1983/Colour)
Banner: B.R.Films
Director: Ravi Chopra
Music Composer: R.D.Burman
Cast: Dilip Kumar, Nanda, Raj Babbar, Padmini Kolhapure, Rati Agnihotri, Raj Kiran & Suresh Oberoi

DUNIYA (1984/Colour)
Banner: Dharma Productions Pvt. Ltd.
Director: Ramesh Talwar
Music Composer: R.D.Burman
Cast: Ashok Kumar (**Mohan Kumar**), Dilip Kumar, Saira Banu, Rishi Kapoor, Amrita Singh, Prem Chopra, Amrish Puri & Pran

MASHAAL (1984/Colour)
Banner: Yash Raj Films
Director: Yash Chopra
Music Composer: Hridaynath Mangeshkar
Cast: Dilip Kumar (**Vinod Kumar**), Waheeda Rehman, Rati Agnihotri, Anil Kapoor, Nilu Phule, Madan Puri, Mohan Agashe, Saeed Jaffrey, Amrish Puri & Iftekar

DHARAM ADHIKARI (1986/Colour)
Banner: U.V.Suryanarayan Rao
Director: K.Raghavendra Rao
Music Composer: Bappi Lahiri
Cast: Dilip Kumar, Jeetendra, Sridevi, Anuradha Patel, Pran, Kader Khan, Shakti Kapoor, Asrani, Rakesh Bedi, Sujit Kumar, Mayur, Rohini Hattangadi, Preeti Sapru & Geeta Siddharth

KARMA (1986/Colour/193 minutes)
Banner: Mukta Arts Pvt. Ltd.
Director: Subhash Ghai
Music Composer: Laxmikant Pyarelal
Cast: Dilip Kumar (**Vishwa Pratap Singh aka Rana**), Nutan, Jackie Shroff, Anil Kapoor, Naseeruddin Shah, Sridevi, Poonam Dhillon, Anupam Kher, Shakti Kapoor, Dara Singh, Satyanarayan & Bindu

KANOON APNA APNA (1989/Colour/162 minutes)
Banner: Madhavi Productions
Director: B.Gopal
Music Composer: Bappi Lahiri
Cast: Dilip Kumar (**Collector Jagat Pratap Singh**), Nutan, Sanjay Dutt, Madhuri Dixit, Kader Khan, Anupam Kher, Gulshan Grover, Tej Sapru, Satyen Kappu, Mayur, Jayashree Gadkar, Meethy, Pinky, Abhilasha, Vijayalakshmi & Disco Shanti

IZZATDAAR (1990/Colour/172 minutes)
Banner: Divya Citizen Combines
Director: K.Bapaiah
Music Composer: Laxmikant Pyarelal
Cast: Dilip Kumar (**Brahm Dutt**), Bharati, Govinda, Madhuri Dixit, Asrani, Tina Ghai, Rakesh Bedi, Dilip Dhavan & Shafi Inamdar

SAUDAGAR (1991/Colour/213 minutes)
Banner: Mukta Arts Pvt Ltd
Director: Subhash Ghai
Music Composer: Laxmikant Pyarelal
Cast: Dilip Kumar (**Veeru Singh**), Raaj Kumar, Jackie Shroff, Manisha Koirala, Vivek Mushran, Deepti Naval, Anupam Kher, Amrish Puri, Gulshan Grover, Dalip Tahil, Mukesh Khanna, Dina Pathak, Anand Balraj, Akash Khurana, Abhinav Chaturvedi, Archana Puran Singh, Malvika Tiwari, Sucheta Vajpai & Shubha Khote

AAG KA DARIYA (completed in 1991 but as yet unreleased/ Colour)
Banner: R.Venkataraman
Director: S.V.Rajendra Singh
Music Composer:
Cast: Dilip Kumar, Rekha, Padmini Kolhapure, Rajiv Kapoor, Amrita Singh and Amrish Puri

KALINGA (1995 but as yet unreleased/Colour)
Banner: Divya Citizen Combines
Director: Dilip Kumar
Music Composer: Kalyanji Anandji
Cast: Dilip Kumar, Raj Babbar, Amjad Khan, Meenakshi Sheshadri, Ammtoje Mann

QILA (1998/Colour)
Banner: Eagle Films
Director: Umesh Mehra
Music Composer: Anand Raj Anand
Cast: Dilip Kumar (double role as **Jagannath Singh** and **Amaranth Singh**), Rekha, Mukul Dev, Mamta Kulkarni, Malay Chakrabarty, Smita Jaykar, Satish Kaushik, Raajeshwari Sachdev and Satish Kaushik

Uncredited Appearances

Dilip Kumar plays himself in the following films:

KALA BAZAAR (1960) as one of the stars attended the star-studded premiere of Mughal-e-Azam where Raghuvir (Dev Anand) is selling tickets in black.

GUDDI (1971) as one of the stars Guddi (Jaya Bachchan) sees when she goes out for shooting.

KOSHISH (1972) as the third man who answers the phone when Haricharan (Sanjeev Kumar) is showing Aarati (Jaya Bachchan) the uses of the instrument.

RAM TERE KITNE NAAM (1985) in a scene from the film *Vidhaata*

Voice Overs

Dilip Kumar also lent his impressive voice to the following films:

DHARAMPUTRA (1961)
NAYA DIN NAYI RAAT (1974)

End of Book Notes 6

– *Little Known Facts about India's Best Known Actor* –

- Dilip Kumar has acted in a total of 60 films plus 3 guest appearances and four uncredited appearances in 54 years (1944-1998). He has never acted in more than 2 to 3 films in a year – hitting the peak at the very beginning with 5 films in 1948. His most productive phase was between 1948 and 1961 when he acted in as many as 31 releases. Between 1964 and 1976 he worked in only 14 films. As a character actor between 1981 and 1998 he has just 14 releases.

- Dilip Kumar has played a Muslim character only once in his entire career: when he comes disguised as Khan Saheb in *Kohinoor*.

- He has never got the National Award for Best Actor though he was awarded the Dadasaheb Phalke Award for Lifetime Achievement in 1995.

- The leading ladies with whom he has been teamed the most are Nargis and Vyjayanthimala (6 times each). The others: Nimmi (5 times), Kamini Kaushal, Madhubala, Meena Kumari, Waheeda Rehman and Saira Banu (4 times each). He has paired only twice with the actress he admired the most, Nalini Jaywant.

- The surprising thing is that he was never paired with Suraiya though they were projected to work in a film named *Janwar*, which was to have been directed by K.Asif.

- He never formed a romantic pair with Nutan in their younger days but starred opposite her in two later films (*Karma* and *Kanoon Apna Apna*). He has also played opposite Rekha in his last two films (*Qila* and *Aag Ka Dariya*).

- Dilip Kumar has acted opposite both his contemporaries at least once: with Raj Kapoor (in *Andaz*) and Dev Anand (in *Insaniyat*). He has acted twice with Raaj Kumar: once in *Paigham* and then again in *Saudagar* (1991). Ditto with Sanjeev Kumar: *Sunghursh* and later *Vidhaata*.

- He has acted in nine films with villain Pran.

- Dilip Kumar has played a double thrice in his film career (*Ram Aur Shyam, Dastaan, Qila*) and a triple role once (*Bairaag*). It is said that he was offered the nine roles of *Naya Din Nayi Raat* (later done by Sanjeev Kumar) but refused to act in the film, settling to speak the commentary.

End of Book Notes 7

– *Awards & Honours* –

1998 Ramnath Goenka Award for contribution in the field of social welfare

1997 Nishan-e-Imtiaz, highest civilian award conferred by the Government of Pakistan

1997 N.T.Rama Rao Award for sterling contribution to Indian cinema

1997 Doctor of Philosophy (Honorary), Guru Nanak University

1995 Dadasaheb Phalke Award for Lifetime Achievement.

1993 Filmfare Lifetime Achievement Award

1991 Padma Bhushan

1982 Filmfare Award Best Actor *(Shakti)*

1967 Filmfare Award Best Actor *(Ram Aur Shyam)*

1964 Filmfare Award Best Actor *(Leader)*

1963 Silver Bowl for Best Film *(Gunga Jumna)*, Boston, USA

1962 Best Actor *(Gunga Jumna)*, Karlovy Vary Film Festival

1960 Filmfare Award Best Actor *(Kohinoor)*

1957 Filmfare Award Best Actor *(Naya Daur)*

1956 Filmfare Award Best Actor *(Devdas)*

1955 Filmfare Award Best Actor *(Azaad)*

1953 Filmfare Award Best Actor *(Daag)*

The award-winners lineup at the 1957 Filmfare Awards: Best Music Director
O P Nayyar (*Naya Daur*), Best Actress Nargis (*Mother India*), Best Actor
Dilip Kumar (*Naya Daur*) and Best Supporting Actress Shyama (*Sharada*);
Saira Banu congratulating husband Dilip Kumar soon after he received the
Dadasaheb Phalke Award in 1995; Dilip Kumar accepting the Doctorate of
Philosophy degree from B K N Chibber, Governor of Punjab, at the 23rd
Annual Convocation of the Guru Nanak University in 1997

– *Bibliography* –

Books

AKBAR, KHATIJA, Madhubala, her Life, Her Times, UBS Publishers, 1997

BHATTACHARYA, RINKI, Bimal Roy: A Man Of Silence, Indus, 1994

BOOCH, HARISH, Star Portraits

IYENGAR, NIRANJAN, The Leader, Junior G, September 1991

LANBA, URMILA, The Life And Films of Dilip Kumar, Vision Books, 2002

MOHANDEEP, The Mystery & Mystic of Madhubala, Magna Books, 1996

REUBEN, BUNNY, Mehboob: India's DeMille, Indus, 1994

Special Issues

Dilip Kumar Special, SCREEN, April 19,1991

Ek Mahanayak Ki Gatha, NAI DUNIYA, December 9, 2002

Articles

BAGDADI, RAFIQUE & RAO, RAJIV Un Lamhon Ne Meri Taqdeer Hi Badal Di, Hindi Screen, March 11, 1994.

BHARATI, RAHI, The Fabulous Loves of Dilip Kumar, Lehren, January 29, 1991

CHUGHTAI, ISMAT, Ab Na Pahale Walwale Hain, Priya, January 1990

DEV ANAND, When Three Was Company, Times of India, October 27, 1991

DILIP KUMAR, What I Want From Life, Filmfare, November 13, 1953

DILIP KUMAR, Brilliant Actor Great Man, Times of India, December 10, 2002

GONSALVES, STARDUST, The Heart Knows Its Own, Screen, February 12, 1993

KANEKAR, SHIRISH, Dilip Kumar: A Photo Feature, Chitranand, Diwali Issue 1978

KHOSLA, S.N., Dilip Kumar Betrays Asma Again, Filmland Times No. 7

KHOSLA, S.N., Unforgettable Dilip Kumar, Movie

MOHAMMED, KHALID, His Basic Instincts, Times of India, June 21, 1992

MOHAMMED, KHALID & KHAN, SALIM, Dilip Kumar: The Tragedy King, Cinema In India, Annual 1992

MOHAMMED, KHALID, A Class Apart, Filmfare, April 1994

MOHAMMED, KHALID, There's No Room for Perverse Religious Fanaticism, Times of India, August 3, 1995

MOHAMMED, KHALID, Sense and Sensibility, Times of India, April 14, 1996

PANJWANI, NARENDRA, Is This Any Way To Live, Times of India, August 6, 1995

RAHEJA, ANITA & AGARWAL, HEENA, Salad Days Are Here Again, Sunday Mid-day August 24, 2003

RAJENDRAN, GIRIJA, Composer steeped in classical idiom

TANWAR, SARITA, Dilip Kumar's Most Heart-rending Interview, Stardust, June 1993

TANWAR, SARITA, I Am An Imposter, Stardust, April 1998

The Dignity Handle of Scandal, Savage Tales of Love, Stardust Classic

Internet

LUTGENDORF, PHILIP, Notes On Indian Popular Cinema, (http://www.uiowa.edu/~incinema/index.html)

RAHEJA, DINESH, Classics Revisited (www.rediff.com)

RMIM ARCHIVES (http://groups.google.co.in)

REDIFF SITE, Dilip Kumar Special (www.rediff.com)

– *Acknowledgements* –

Though the author puts his name on the cover and the publisher abets him in this act, the writing of a book is rarely the task of one person alone. Several others help out with information, criticism and plain moral support. Among those who helped me are:

- **SHAHABUDDIN M.ISMAIL** who gave me full and unconditional access to his valuable library of rare newspaper and magazine clippings on Dilip Kumar, without which the detailing of this book would have been impossible.
- **KIRAN SHANTARAM** for allowing me access to old issues of Film India and other books at the multi-lingual library of the Dr V.Shantaram Motion Picture Foundation.
- **SAYED AMJAD HUSSAIN** of Ohio, USA for allowing me to use his excellent map of old-time Peshawar which shows the street and mohalla in which Dilip Kumar was born and lived as a child.
- **D.B.SAMANT** for his valuable insights into the era and particularly sharing with me his extensive knowledge of film music.
- **R.M.KUMTAKAR**, my older colleague at Screen, now deceased, who introduced me to many of the veterans cited here in the book.
- **BADRI PRASAD JOSHI, JEJE THAKUR & NOOR ALI MERCHANT** for locating some rare photos and video cassettes of Dilip Kumar starrers.
- **V.A.K.RANGA RAO and SURJIT SINGH**
- **the innumerable film journalists** who interviewed and wrote on Dilip Kumar.

and, of course ….
- **R.K.MEHRA, INDIRA KHANNA, SAYANTANI DASGUPTA, KAPIL GUPTA** and the entire staff at Rupa & Co. for their constant encouragement and help.